EVERYDAY HISTORY

LIFE IN

ANCIENT EGYPT

SARAH RIDLEY

This edition 2010

First published in 2007
by Franklin Watts

Copyright © Franklin Watts 2007

Franklin Watts
338 Euston Road
London NW1 3BH

Franklin Watts Australia
Level 17/207 Kent Street
Sydney, NSW 2000

A CIP catalogue record for this book is available from the British Library.

ISBN 978 0 7496 9613 9

Printed in Malaysia

Franklin Watts is a division of
Hachette Children's Books, an Hachette UK company.
www.hachette.co.uk

The text of this book is based on
Clues to the Past – Everyday Life in Ancient Egypt
by Nathaniel Harris
Copyright © Franklin Watts 1994

Picture credits:
Courtesy of the Trustees of the British Museum, London:
front cover bl, 6t, 10t, 12t, 12-13b, 14t, 16t, 18t, 20t, 22t, 26t.
Werner Forman Archive: 4t, 7b, 8t, 24t, 28t.
Michael Holford: 6b, 30r.
Hulton Deutsch Collection: 7t.

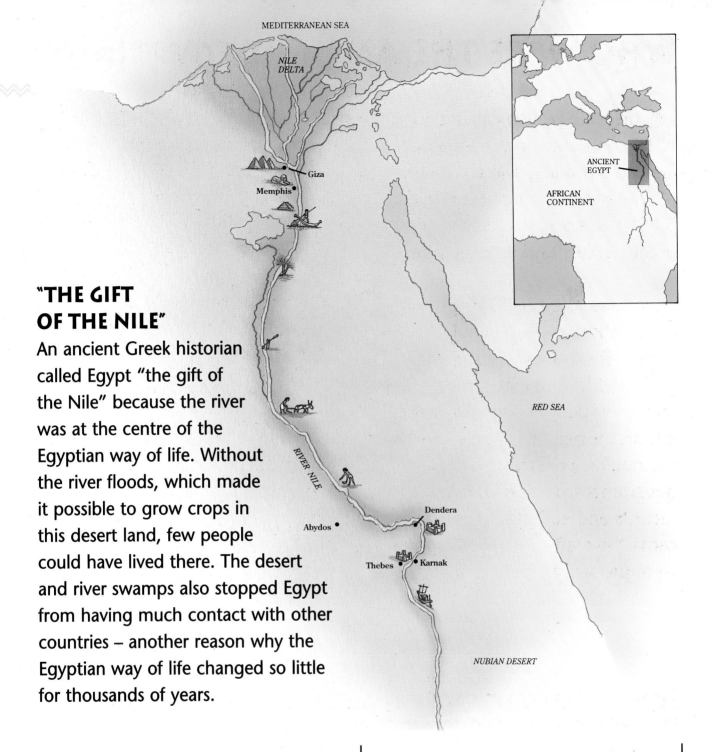

MEDITERRANEAN SEA

NILE DELTA

Giza

Memphis

ANCIENT EGYPT

AFRICAN CONTINENT

RED SEA

RIVER NILE

Dendera

Abydos

Thebes • Karnak

NUBIAN DESERT

"THE GIFT OF THE NILE"

An ancient Greek historian called Egypt "the gift of the Nile" because the river was at the centre of the Egyptian way of life. Without the river floods, which made it possible to grow crops in this desert land, few people could have lived there. The desert and river swamps also stopped Egypt from having much contact with other countries – another reason why the Egyptian way of life changed so little for thousands of years.

New Kingdom

1567 BCE The Hyksos are driven out.

1458 BCE Tuthmosis III conquers Syria and Palestine.

1350 BCE The pharaoh Akhenaten attempts to set up a new supreme god, the Aten.

1323 BCE The death of Tutankhamun, famous because of the discovery of his tomb in 1922.

Late Period

525 BCE Egypt is conquered by the Persians.

332 BCE Alexander the Great of Greece conquers Egypt.

323–30 BCE The Ptolemies rule as pharaohs.

30 BCE Egypt becomes part of the Roman Empire.

5

HOW DO WE KNOW ABOUT THE ANCIENT EGYPTIANS?

We know a great deal about the ancient Egyptians because large numbers of their records, pictures and personal possessions have survived. One reason for this is that the hot, dry climate has preserved objects that would normally rot away, like bodies, paper and wood. Equally important is the ancient Egyptians' belief in life after death which meant that they put all sorts of objects into tombs with their dead.

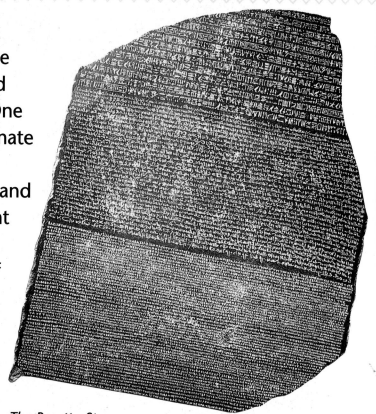

The Rosetta Stone, discovered in 1799.

IMMENSE STRUCTURES

Egypt is full of huge structures such as pyramids, temples and obelisks (tall stone monuments). The pyramids were built as gigantic tombs for Egypt's pharaohs.

The pyramid at Chephren, built c. 2570 BCE.

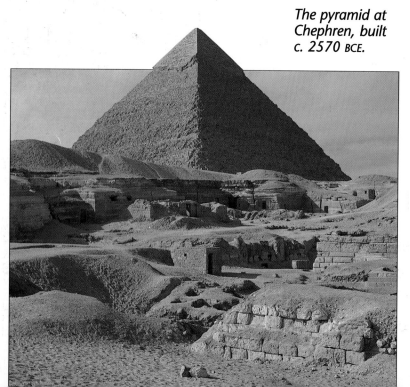

WRITTEN EVIDENCE

The ancient Egyptians left behind them writings of many types but, as their language had died out, no one knew how to read it until the discovery of the Rosetta Stone (*above*). Scholars realised that the stone was engraved with three versions of the same text – one in ancient Greek and two in different forms of Egyptian writing. Using the Greek, the Frenchman Jean Francois Champollion, was able to understand the Egyptian writing, and in time the whole language was decoded.

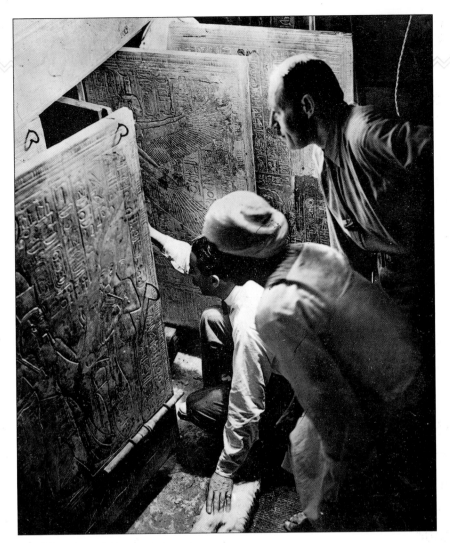

ARCHAEOLOGISTS AT WORK

Archaeologists dig up the buried past and are often as interested in rubbish tips as in valuable objects. In 1922 Howard Carter, a British archaeologist, discovered the tomb of the pharaoh, Tutankhamun, packed with priceless ancient Egyptian treasures. It had not been disturbed since it was sealed up 3,000 years before.

Howard Carter (at the front) opens the entrance into the fourth chamber of Tutankhamun's tomb.

PAINTING AND SCULPTURE

Many paintings have survived on the walls of tombs or temples, or inside books. They show all sorts of scenes and activities from ancient Egyptian life.

Enormous sculptures also survive, alongside tomb monuments, which often show affectionate couples and groups. The Egyptians also placed many small wooden or stone statues inside tombs, to represent the dead person's wealth and pleasures.

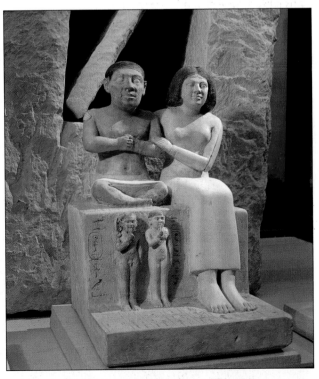

A tomb monument showing a family.

ON THE RIVER NILE

Almost all ancient Egyptians lived close to the River Nile. They would have watched wooden sailing boats, similar to this model found in a tomb, carrying people and goods up and down the river. Where the river was shallow, a sailor used a weight on the end of a piece of rope to check the depth.

LIFE-GIVING FLOOD

The River Nile made a strip of land either side of the river fertile enough to grow good crops. In mid-June, the river flooded and when the water level fell again four months later, it left a thick layer of mud behind it. The wheat and barley crops grown in this soil were used to make bread and beer, the main foods in the Egyptian diet.

The River Nile is about 5,600 km long. As it gets close to the sea, it splits up into several branches in the flat Delta area.

Young men hunt a hippo. This was dangerous work as the animal could easily upset the boat.

8

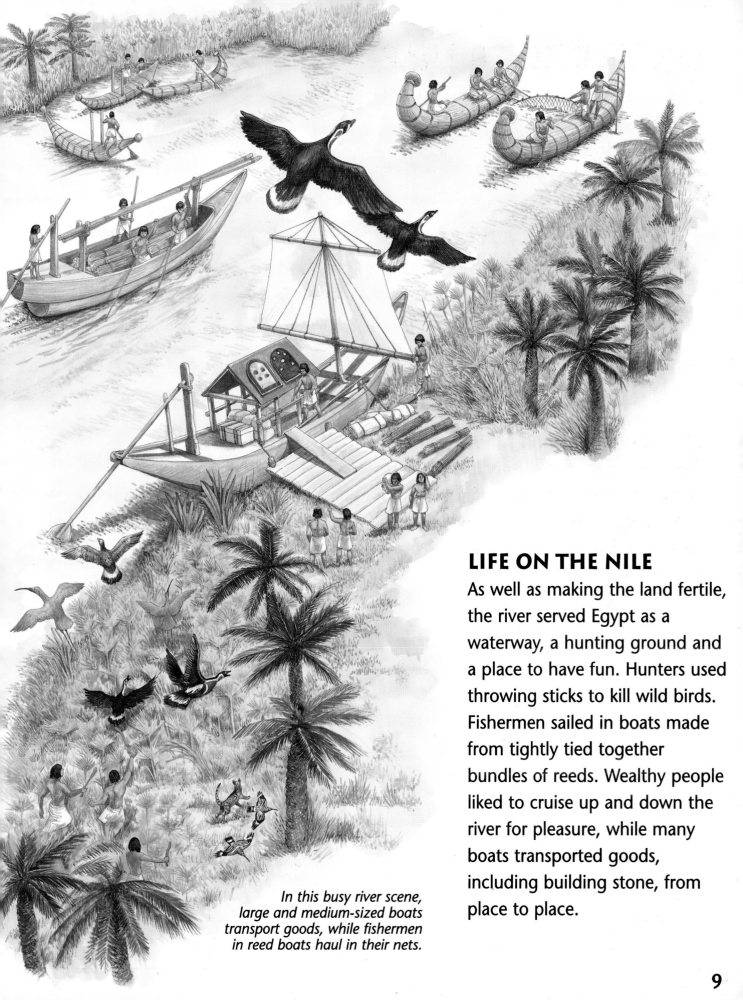

LIFE ON THE NILE

As well as making the land fertile, the river served Egypt as a waterway, a hunting ground and a place to have fun. Hunters used throwing sticks to kill wild birds. Fishermen sailed in boats made from tightly tied together bundles of reeds. Wealthy people liked to cruise up and down the river for pleasure, while many boats transported goods, including building stone, from place to place.

In this busy river scene, large and medium-sized boats transport goods, while fishermen in reed boats haul in their nets.

LIVING WITH ANIMALS

The ancient Egyptians lived close to animals of all kinds. Their most valuable farm animals were cattle. In this tomb painting (*right*) government workers record how many cattle each herder owns to work out the amount of tax the herder must pay to the government.

FRIENDS AND NEIGHBOURS

The ancient Egyptians seem to have been fond of animals. Wall paintings show them stroking animals and many kept dogs, cats and monkeys as pets. Farm animals lived in stables and stalls close to the house, while poor families often shared their one living room with their cow or other animal.

Animals were linked to gods and goddesses (see pages 28-29). For example, Hathor, the goddess of love and music, was usually shown as a cow. The Egyptians also mummified some of their animals so that they could survive into the afterlife (see page 30).

OUT IN THE DESERT

Most Egyptians feared the desert, a dangerous place full of wild animals. However kings and their rich friends liked to hunt some of the wild animals, including lions, wild bulls, elephants and even ostriches. Camels roamed wild in the desert and were not tamed until late in ancient Egyptian history.

Egypt's riverbanks, marshes and the areas on the edge of the desert were rich in wildlife. Here a hunter returns with a desert hare and a young deer.

Herders attend to cattle on a large estate – milking them and helping one to give birth.

Birds such as geese (below) were force-fed – made to swallow too much food – in order to fatten them up for eating.

Table

BEASTS FOR USE AND FOOD

There were large herds of cattle on big farms. The landowners grew fields of clover and other crops specially for them to eat. At night the herders brought the cattle safely back to the cattlesheds, away from wild animals. Poor farmers owned few cattle but raised goats, pigs or chickens instead.

The Egyptians used their animals to work for them, pulling ploughs and carts or carrying goods to market.

WORKING IN THE FIELDS

After the floods, farmers ploughed in the rich, fertile mud using wooden ploughs similar to the one shown in this model found in a tomb (*right*). Every scrap of land flooded by the river was used to grow crops as most of Egypt was desert.

THE FARMER'S YEAR

The Nile floods took over farmers' lives. In the autumn, after the floods, they ploughed and sowed the seeds. Then in March it was harvest time, perhaps followed by planting a second crop of vegetables before the next flood. During the floods, farmers could relax unless they were called up to help build temples and pyramids. Another important job was to maintain the canals and ditches used to bring water to the crops during the dry season.

The boundaries (edges) of a farmer's fields were marked with large stones. Government officials inspected the fields before every harvest to make sure no one had been tempted to move the boundary stones.

2   1

MAKING WINE
You need to read each of these Egyptian picture strips from right to left. The first strip shows grapes being picked from vines (1) and carried away (2).

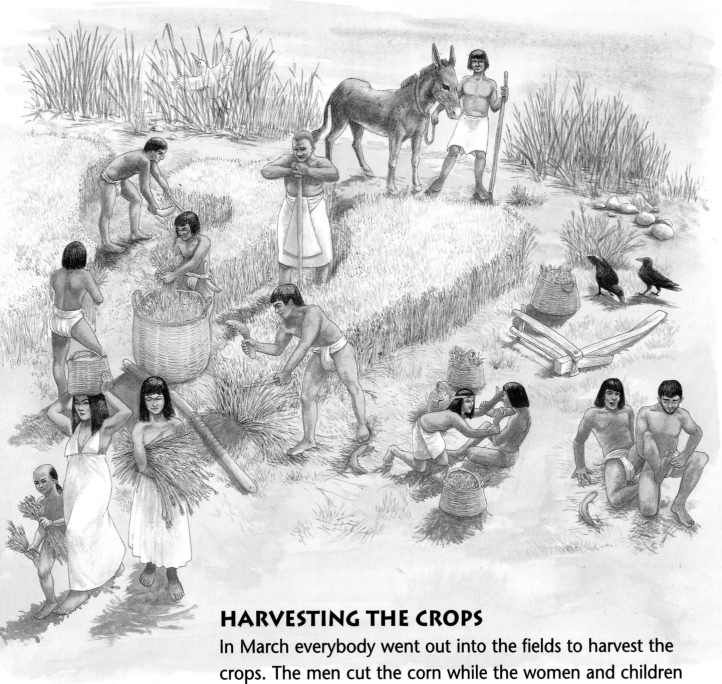

HARVESTING THE CROPS

In March everybody went out into the fields to harvest the crops. The men cut the corn while the women and children packed it into baskets. Some people searched the ground to pick up any corn that had fallen down.

Villagers harvest corn by hand – hot work under the blazing sun.

4

3

Here (3) the grapes are being trampled with bare feet to release the juice, which is stored in jars and left to turn into wine (4).

CRAFTSMEN

Skilled craftsmen made many beautiful objects and pieces of furniture, some of which have survived to this day. This jewellery (*right*) was worn around the waist of a wealthy woman. It was thought to bring her good luck, good health and many children. The metal parts are made of electrum, a mixture of gold and silver.

SKILLS ABOUND

Craftsmen of all types worked in towns and villages, building houses or making pots, baskets, furniture, jewellery or metal objects. The pharaohs employed huge numbers of craftsmen to build their tombs, carve statues, paint wall paintings and fill the tombs with fantastic objects for them to enjoy in the afterlife.

The ancient Egyptians made many beautiful objects from glass, and covered pottery objects, such as this hippo, with glass glaze.

Metalworkers in a busy workshop.

A carpenter's tools. The adze was used to scrape wood smooth.

Adze

Saw

Drill

METALWORK

The Egyptians liked copper and bronze and preferred them even after they knew about iron, a much tougher metal. Metalworkers only made solid gold objects for the pharaohs and the temples but many other objects were gilded, which means they were covered in a thin layer of gold.

THE POWER OF WORDS

The pharaoh ruled the people of Egypt with the help of a huge number of government officials who kept many records. Scribes (professional writers) wrote the records using reed pens and black and red ink. The palette (*right*) held pens and blocks of ink. The scribe ground the ink into powder and added water.

Palette

Grinder

Water pot

MANY DUTIES

Since most people could not read or write, they paid a scribe to write letters for them. Some scribes had more demanding jobs as they recorded each farmer's harvest and worked out how much tax he must pay to the pharaoh.

Others helped organise big projects, such as building temples and pyramids, or they worked in the army, keeping good records and calculating how much food and other materials everyone needed.

SOME HIEROGLYPHICS

TYPES OF WRITING

There were three types of writing: hieroglyphics, hieratic and demotic. The hieratic and demotic writing systems were simplified forms of hieroglyphics which scribes could use to write quickly.

There were over 700 hieroglyphs, each like a little drawing. Some were pictures of the thing they stood for, while others represented sounds or groups of letters.

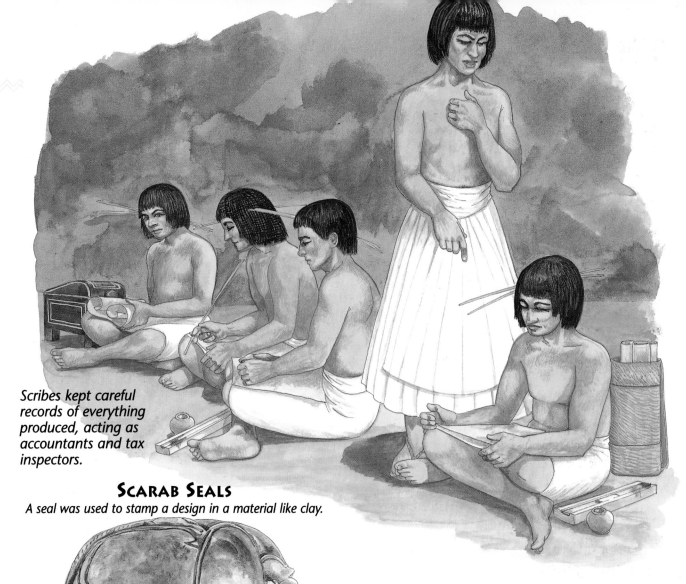

Scribes kept careful records of everything produced, acting as accountants and tax inspectors.

SCARAB SEALS

A seal was used to stamp a design in a material like clay.

Some seals were made to mark a great event, such as the birth of a royal prince.

This one tells of a great lion hunt.

SCRIBES AT WORK

A scribe was often the son of a scribe, learning his skills from his father. But as more and more of them were needed, schools were set up to train young men. As well as hieroglyphics and hieratic writing, they learned subjects like arithmetic, useful for people who would spend a lot of their working lives recording numbers and making calculations. Scribes wrote down information on lengths of papyrus (a type of paper made from reeds), which rolled up like wallpaper.

EGYPT AT WAR

The army was organised into foot soldiers and chariot troops. The battle-axe (*right*) was a fearsome weapon carried by the foot soldiers. It has a bronze axe head and a strong wooden handle. Certain craftsmen devoted themselves to making weapons in workshops that were almost like small factories.

LATECOMERS TO WAR

For over a thousand years, the Egyptians were peaceable and only formed an army if they were being attacked. This changed around 3000 BCE when the Egyptians decided to attack and take over parts of Nubia, a country to the south of Egypt. Then, in 1780 BCE, Egypt itself was invaded by the Hyksos from Asia. For two hundred years the Egyptians fought battles to try to push the Hyksos out again. During this time, the army became well organised. Egypt went on to fight wars and win land in Syria and Palestine.

Foot soldiers fought their enemies hand to hand with battle-axes, spears, knives and clubs, while protecting themselves with their shields.

Sword

Dagger

Bow and arrows

Spear   Shield

The army advances. The chariot drivers ran down the enemy's foot soldiers or surrounded the entire enemy army and attacked from behind.

After a victory the Egyptians cut off the right hand of their dead enemies and counted them, to see how many they had killed. Lucky prisoners were forced to join the Egyptian army. Unlucky ones had their hands chopped off, or were sold to be slaves.

CHARIOTS

The Egyptians used chariots pulled by a pair of horses in battle. Pharaohs are often shown in wall-paintings standing alone in their chariots. In fact, there were usually two people in the chariot – the driver and an archer, who fired arrows at the enemy.

HOUSES AND HOMES

Houses were made from mud bricks, as stone was only used to build temples and tombs. This model found in a tomb (*right*) shows the type of home where an ordinary Egyptian family would have lived. Model houses like these were placed in tombs to be the dead person's home after death.

HOME COMFORTS

Very poor people lived in reed huts but most people lived in one- or two-storey homes with several rooms. When a new house was built, it was finished with a coat of plaster and wall-paintings inside. The windows were small to keep out the heat. Wealthy people owned town and country homes with gardens designed around pools.

Most people had no furniture except a chest and some mats. The rich owned elegant chairs, stools, small tables and beds.

Neighbours chat over the wall that divides their houses.

MAKING BRICKS

Mud was mixed with straw, or sometimes sand, to add strength. Then it was packed into hollow, brick-shaped wooden moulds. These were left to bake in the hot sun.

TOWNS

Most Egyptian towns grew up, unplanned, around temples or palaces. The poor lived in small houses crowded into a maze of streets. Wealthier people lived in larger homes often built on several floors, as it was expensive to build a house that took up a lot of ground space. The roof provided an extra storage place and, more importantly, somewhere for the family to relax and catch the cooling breeze.

FOOD AND DRINK

The Nile floods meant that the Egyptians were able to grow enough food for everyone. Poorer people ate a simple diet of bread, vegetables and fish. Richer people could choose from more exciting foods, especially at banquets like the one shown in the wall-painting (*right*), which shows cakes, baskets of figs, meat and plenty of wine.

THE EGYPTIAN DIET

The main crops of wheat and barley were made into bread and beer. Written records mention 17 different kinds of beer and 50 types of bread, as well as pastries and cakes. Since there was no sugar, wealthier Egyptians used honey or the juice of figs and dates to sweeten food.

The Egyptians liked strong-tasting vegetables, like onions and garlic, and believed they were good for health. They also ate peas, beans, lettuces, cucumbers and leeks. Figs, dates and grapes were favourite fruits but only the well-off drank wine. Ordinary people ate fish, chicken and wild birds. The rich preferred beef and exotic meats such as antelope.

Some fish was dried, to provide food for another time. People hung up the fish to bake in the hot sun and then packed them in ash to help preserve them.

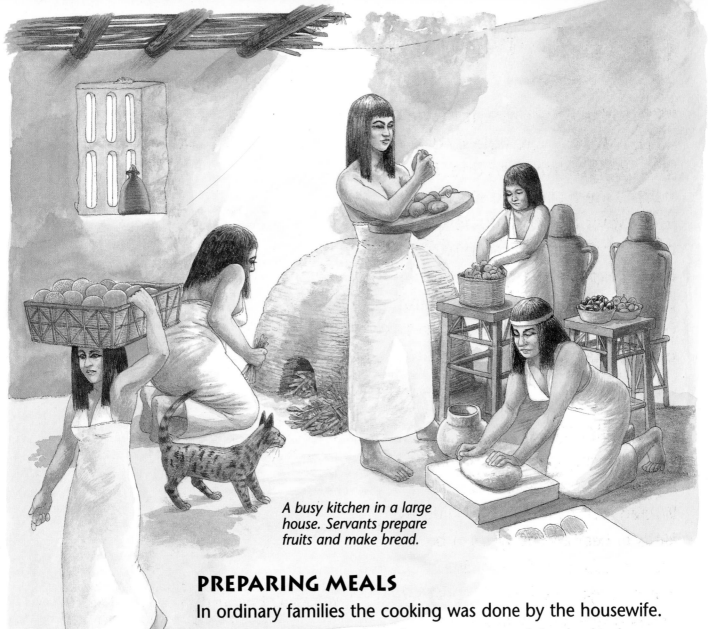

A busy kitchen in a large house. Servants prepare fruits and make bread.

PREPARING MEALS

In ordinary families the cooking was done by the housewife. Wealthy families employed servants to work in the kitchen and a chef to do the cooking. The Egyptians had ovens and also knew how to boil, roast and fry food.

MAKING BREAD

The first step in bread-making was to grind the corn into flour.

The flour was mixed with water, yeast and salt to make dough. This was kneaded and left for a time to rise.

Then the dough was baked in a small oven.

CLOTHES AND FASHION

Most of the time, Egypt was so hot that people wore as little as possible. The wealthy women shown in this wall-painting (*right*) have dressed up for a banquet. They are wearing stylish wigs, wide collars and pleated dresses. Each has a cone of scented fat on her head that will slowly melt in the heat, to cool the head while releasing a pleasant smell.

DRESS SENSE

Children rarely wore clothes, while working people and servants often worked almost naked. Most men were content to wear a simple white kilt (short pleated skirt), while women wore long, close-fitting shift dresses. The wealthiest people wore similar clothes but had the clothes pleated and added a light, sometimes see-through, cloak on the top.

In contrast to their simple clothes, people wore elaborate wigs and all sorts of extras – headbands, necklaces, collars, belts, bracelets and rings.

HAIR AND WIGS

Men and women wore their hair short, and men hardly ever wore beards. Priests shaved their heads completely. Men and women wore wigs, especially on important occasions. Professional wigmakers sold wigs made in their workshops.

Applicators

A wealthy lady does her make-up at the beginning of another day.

Face-cream pot

Bronze mirror

THE QUEST FOR BEAUTY

Wealthy women did everything they could to make themselves look beautiful. They bathed often and used creams and perfumes. There was plenty of make-up to choose from, especially for the eyes. Kohl, a black material, was used to outline the eyes and to darken the lashes and eyebrows.

Egyptian ladies had a variety of beauty aids which they carried around with them in cosmetic boxes.

Perfume pot

25

MUSIC, DANCE AND GAMES

Children and adults relaxed by playing games, music and sport. Some children's toys have survived the thousands of years since an Egyptian child played with them. They include this wooden cat, with its movable jaw. The child pulled the string to make the jaw move.

SPORTS AND GAMES

Most sports and games were simple and easy to set up. Boys went in for all sorts of running, jumping and fighting but seem to have left ball games to the girls. With water never far away, everyone enjoyed swimming. Wealthy people hunted for pleasure (see page 10) and raced their chariots. Ordinary men competed against each other in athletics, wrestling and archery competitions.

Board games were popular, especially *senet* which was played by everyone, from pharaohs down to workers.

Here are drawings of a few of the toys found by archaeologists. The wooden horse has a hole through its nose for a string, so that it could be pulled along. Children wound string round the spinning tops or twisted them into action with their fingers.

Clay balls

Pull-along horse

Spinning tops

A rich couple sit by the pool in their garden while the children play with their toys.

ENTERTAINMENT

Villagers often met to sing and make music, but when there was dancing, men and women never performed together. As the Egyptians had no way of writing down their music, we do not know how it sounded.

At parties, dancing girls, acrobats and musicians entertained the guests.

Many Egyptians played flutes and pipes to make their own music. Wealthy people employed harpists, trumpeters and lyre-players to accompany singers at parties. Rattles, cymbals and drums beat out the rhythm for dancers.

Cymbals

Flute

Lyre

RELIGION

The ancient Egyptians worshipped hundreds of gods and goddesses, each one connected to a different side of life or death. Many were represented by animals, or by human beings with animal heads. This statue (*right*) shows the sky god, Horus the Elder, as a falcon. It still stands today outside the Temple of Horus in Edfu, Egypt.

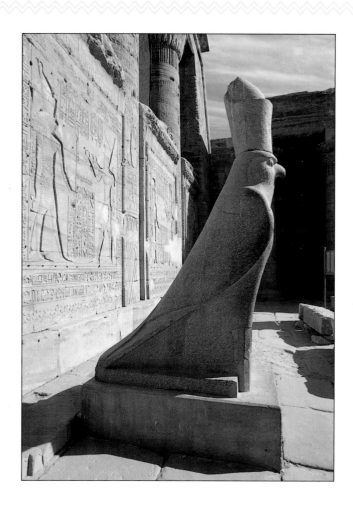

Egyptians used amulets (below) to protect against certain dangers or to give themselves particular strengths or powers. Some represented a god, like the eye of Horus, while others were in the shape of a hieroglyph (see page 16).

LAND OF MANY GODS

The greatest of all the gods was Re, the life-giving sun god. He was believed to be the father of the pharaoh, seen as a living god, who represented the god Horus on earth.

The ancient Egyptians thought it was important to worship the gods and goddesses and keep them happy so that life would continue well on Earth.

A religious procession moves through the inner courtyard of a temple to the god Horus. A statue of Horus is inside the golden box.

The sistrum was a metal rattle used by priestesses during religious ceremonies.

Sistrum

TEMPLES

Egypt was a land of mighty temples, built at the command of the pharaoh. Temples were busy places, with schools, workshops, granaries and libraries. Only the priests and priestesses were allowed into the heart of the temple – the sanctuary where the god lived. They cared for the god's image every day but only brought it out to the people on special festival days.

THE AFTERLIFE

The Egyptians believed in life after death. As it was vital that the body should survive for this afterlife, it was mummified. This meant it was given a special treatment, called embalming, to stop it from decaying. The mummified body was then placed inside a coffin, like this one (*right*) for a priestess. A painter created a portrait of the dead person on the outside of the coffin.

MAKING A MUMMY

Mummification was skilled work, carried out by priestly embalmers. In the workshop they removed the internal organs, dried them out and placed them in *canopic* jars (*see right*). Then they packed the body with the chemical natron, which dried and preserved it. Finally they wrapped the body in bandages and covered the face with a mask.

Little wooden figures called shabtis *were placed in the tomb. If the dead person was ordered to do any work in the afterlife, he, or she, could get the shabtis to do it instead!*

BACK TO LIFE

Just before the dead person was laid in the tomb, the priests performed the "opening of the mouth" ceremony. They stood the coffin upright and touched its face with various objects. They believed this brought the mummy back to life, allowing it to breathe and enjoy the afterlife.

As the mourners wail, a priest prepares to perform the "opening of the mouth" ceremony.

These human and animal-headed jars, called canopic jars, held the dead person's internal organs – the intestines, stomach, liver and lungs. They were placed in the tomb alongside the body.

INDEX

Joan Miró – a preface

Miró refused to comment, despite the heated debate that was going on. Max
Ernst grabbed a coil of rope, while others pinioned Miró's arms. The noose was
laid around his neck and he was threatened with the death penalty for keeping
? mouth shut. Still, he remained quiet.
    do not know what the fight was about. Later, when the artist and photo-
    Man Ray made a portrait of Miró, he placed a piece of rope in the back-
    snickering reference to the prank.[1]
s Miró's close friend, the poet Michel Leiris, explained in an interview after
ró's death in 1983, the Surrealist circle had a tendency to mock Miró a little
bit. Miró was the picture of bourgeois reserved correctness. He worked in a
    ly disciplined way and was not a womanizer. He insisted on leaving the
    tural centre Paris and returning regularly to his native Catalonia,
    ditions, landscape and art moulded his spiritual life and reserved per-
    Also, Miró's images were considered by many to be naive or childlike.
    noose was laid around his neck, it was directed at least partly seri-
    inst the man who lived what could only be called an anti-bohemian
    joke about the hanging could not have happened with anybody else.
    was afraid that they would hang him. His main quality lay in his
    spoke very little; he spoke a little about his projects but stopped
    later in 1947, when Miró – by then a renowned artist – took his
    United States and met the famous art critic, Clement Greenberg,
    ach the same frustration in his audience. Greenberg: "Those who
    rtunity to meet Miró while he was here saw a short, compact,
    man in a dark blue business suit. He has a neat round head with
    med dark hair, pale skin, small, regular features, quick eyes and
    He is slightly nervous and at the same time impersonal in the com-
    ngers, and his conversation and manner are non-commital to an ex-
    sked oneself what could have brought this bourgeois to modern
    Left Bank, and Surrealism."[3]
    iró does become intimate with his audience through his paintings,
    h are full of sex, humour, nature, excrement, playfulness, and sometimes
    and anger. He expanded painting to the point where it intersects with the
    of poetry. It was a poetry born of hard work, for work – not the societal
    he art world – was the most important part of his life. He was a
    ary painter who tried to work like a labourer with a family to support.
    gh his mature art is based on his own highly personal experience of the
    rld, it reaches out to mythic dimensions, touching upon universal essences
    ad rhythms. That must sound rather vague to someone without a picture of
Miró's to look at and illustrate the point. The best thing would be to see what
this man painted, and how it came about.

Man Ray
Portrait of Joan Miró, around 1930
This portrait by Man Ray plays upon an event
that took place in a studio in Paris: when Miró
refused to make any comment during a debate,
his neighbour Max Ernst grabbed a coil of
rope, placed a noose around his neck and
threatened him with the death sentence should
he give no answer. Miró remained silent.

Self-Portrait, 1917
The picture from 1917 is the earliest self-portrait by Joan Miró. Apart from one dated to
1919, this is the only picture depicting Miró
as a young man.

"If this is painting, then I am Velázquez."

Joan Miró became an artist under relatively hostile conditions. It was the kind of hostility that greets almost every young artist when he or she tries to resist the predictable parental suggestion of entering any respectable and safe profession. But it was also the hostility of an aged art world that had locked itself into its own academies and was getting furious at the youngsters who were starting to climb out of the windows. Born in 1893 in Barcelona, Miró belonged to a generation faced with the inheritance of the ninteenth century "isms" that had liberated painting from its job of depicting recognizable subjects. However, by the time Miró was ready to open the door of the art world, Cubism had already disassembled and reconstructed the picture space and its subject matter and Dada had just dynamited art's meaning. The Fauves had stopped using paint to show nature, and had begun using nature to show paint. In short, the academic art world was under attack and some enemy camps had already formed. Young artists had to decide about their allegiance. Then they had to find their own artistic identities. The war going on in the art world was, in its way, a picture of the greater institutional decay and the struggle for a new order within the world's political balance. For example in Spain, the government changed 44 times between 1898 and 1923.

Joan Miró's national identity was clear to him from the very beginning, which is more than can be said for his artistic identity. He was a Catalan, not a "Spanish" citizen. His father was a goldsmith and watchmaker from Tarragona, whose own father had been a blacksmith. (Miró was named "Joan" after this grandfather.) Miró's father left his native village for Barcelona, where he switched to precious metals and built up a very successful business. Miró's mother was the daughter of a cabinet-maker from Palma de Majorca, whom grandson Joan never met. The cabinet-maker could not read or write and spoke only the Majorquin dialect, yet he managed to advance from an assistant carpenter to the owner of a successful business. He also loved to travel and got as far as Russia by train, "which at that time was really something." His wife, Miró's grandmother, was "very intelligent and romantic"[4]. Miró had an extremely close, if not conflict-free relationship with his family. He writes about his parents, "My mother had a strong personality and was very intelligent. I was always very close to her. She cried when she saw I was on the wrong track. But later, she took a great interest in my work. My father was very realistic and absolutely the opposite of my mother. When I went hunting with him, if I said the sky was purple he made fun of me, which threw me into a rage."[5] Although both hailed from a background of craftsmen, Miró's parents had an extremely low

Miró amongst a group of students from Francesc D'A. Galí's academy, around 1912–14 (3rd from left)

The Farmer, around 1912–1914
Miró's first works are strongly influenced by modern art; particularly by the work of van Gogh and the Fauves. Traces of this influence can be found in the heavy brush strokes of this early oil painting.

The Corn Doctor, 1901

Jewellery design: *Rolled-up snake,* 1908

Peacock, 1908

opinion of the profession of painting pictures ("wrong track") and kept him on a short financial leash. Miró remembers his sister fondly because she slipped him money when he "didn't have a cent to buy paints…"[6]

A reserved and dreamy child of fragile health, Miró was a poor student at school. He remembered being somewhat better at geography – something flat and pictorial – than at other subjects like the practical sciences, but even in geography he let himself be guided by a second sense instead of knowledge: "… Often I guessed precisely the answer to the professor's question by pointing a stick at the map at random."[7] Miró started drawing classes at the age of seven. During the very same year he began what became an annual trip to his grandparents, thus exchanging the city of Barcelona for more provincial Catalan surroundings. The inhabitants were simple farmers. His maternal grandmother lived on Majorca. Miró travelled there by ship, accompanied by a household servant; those trips taught him to love the sea. While the countryside visits were meant to help improve his health, those summer trips probably also freed Miró of a great many parental restrictions. He was a visitor, an observer, and he spent a lot of time drawing by himself. The many sketchbooks Miró saved from his youth show accurate, if unremarkable, observations of village streets and architecture, as if he were memorizing the places he saw. Later as an adult, he would continue to return to the countryside of his childhood for long periods, usually during the summer and fall. In 1907, when Miró was only fourteen years old, the question of his future career loomed against the horizon line marked by the unsuccessful end of his secondary schooling. His father firmly suggested business classes. He attended them. But he also simultaneously attended the famous art academy "La Escuela de la Lonja", where Picasso's father had taught and Picasso himself had been briefly enrolled nine years earlier. Unlike Picasso, who had already mastered the techniques of academic painting with amazing ease at the same age, Miró was still a raw beginner showing no particular promise. He studied with Modesto Urgell Inglada, a painter of melancholy landscapes somewhat in the style of Arnold Böcklin, and José Pasco Merisa, a professor of the decorative and applied arts. The latter suited Miró's father, since he would have also liked to have seen his son become interested in the goldsmith trade. Urgell's horizons, his subject matter of landscapes with the heavens above them, left an impression on Miró and would recur in some of his later painting. Pasco, on the other hand, taught Miró to be as free as possible in his work, to trust and follow his own inclinations. As a whole, the decorative arts were a field free of perspective and illusionistic space, where Miró could relax into expressiveness. When Pasco directed his students' interest to the colourful vitality of Catalan folk crafts, Miró must have felt released from academicism into the warm pool of his love for the Catalan heritage.

After the seventeen-year-old Miró had completed his business schooling, he began a job as book-keeper for Dalmau Oliveres, a hardware and chemical company, and put his artwork aside. This led to a minor nervous breakdown followed by a bout with Typhoid fever, which finally convinced his father that he was not suited for business and office work. Miró later writes about this period in his life, "Fights with the family; give up painting to work in an office. – Catastrophe; do drawings on account books and am fired, naturally. At nineteen I enter the Galí Academy in Barcelona to devote myself entirely to painting. A marvel of awkwardness and incompetence."[8] The private academy led by Francesc D'A. Galí was very progressive. Galí did not ascribe to any particular

Paul Cézanne
Still Life with Apples and Oranges,
1895–1900

Henri Matisse
The Red Serving Table, 1908

direction of modern art, but tried to create an atmosphere that would help each student on his or her individual way. A sort of anti-professor, Galí would take his students on walks in the mountains and forbid them to sketch; instead, they were supposed to use their eyes alone to burn their impressions into their memories. Music was also an important element in the school, where there was a concert every Saturday, as well as a choir. In the concerts of the Society for Chamber Music that Galí had founded in Barcelona, his students had reserved box seats. These activities brought the reserved Miró together with fellow students, several of which were to remain his best friends for his whole life. One of them was Llorens Artigas, the ceramicist with whom he would collaborate on many big projects after the Second World War.

Interestingly enough, Miró credits two of his professors with using the same method to teach him, which either means they both did, or that he fused their teachings in his mind because this method had become his most important recollection of student days. Both Pasco at La Lonja and Galí supposedly had him draw objects which he was not allowed to see. Miró would hold an object behind his back and then try to reproduce its appearance inspired by tactile impressions alone. For Miró, this was an important lesson in his battle of mastering form.[9] Although he considered himself a successful colourist, he was bitterly unhappy with the way he could depict objects. The concept of initially disregarding the way things looked seemed to sharpen his feel for what he could accept

Vincent van Gogh
Le Père Tanguy, around 1887

Claude Monet
La Japonaise (Camille Monet in Japanese Costume), 1876

Ill. p. 13:
***Portrait of E.C. Ricart,* 1917**
Like van Gogh and Monet, Miró refers to Japanese art with his portrait of his studio-mate. He has incorporated a Japanese print in the background, whose delicate lines are almost crushed by the bold forms and colours of the figure. In this way, Miró contrasts and combines East Asian and modern art in one picture.

as a correct form for his composition. It kept the real look of something from distracting him. It also helped Miró to escape obedient copying and freed his power of invention, as well as strengthening his sculptural sense.

Miró's father was always checking up with Galí to make sure his son was making progress. As Galí later told Miró's biographer, Jacques Dupin, "He was a pleasant man… a typical Catalan businessman who was concerned with the 'deals' and material advantages of life. Every week I repeated, 'Your son will be successful, he will be a great artist'…"[10] Although Miró's family was in good financial circumstances, they did not intend to support Miró all too generously in his resolution to become an artist. Obviously, they still thought he should be financially independent of them and have some sort of profession. "In order to earn a living and paint at the same time, my family advised me to become a monk or a soldier…"[11] At that time in Spain, every young man was required to fulfill military service unless he paid his way out. Miró's father was willing to pay only part of the sum that would have entirely exempted his son. In 1915, Miró entered the military in Barcelona for an abbreviated stint, and fulfilled his required service for three months of every year through till 1917. He spent the remaining part of the year working in a studio in Barcelona that he shared with E.C. Ricart, a friend he had got to know at the Academy Galí, and in Montroig, a village in the province of Tarragona where his family had bought a farm in 1911.

Montroig became a centre of authenticity against which Miró measured the power of his art. The Catalan farmers and their families, the animals, insects, trees, rocks and soil were linked together in an animistic world that seemed to Miró to be a mirror of creation itself. Like many other artists of his generation, Miró wanted to express something eternal and essential, and he looked to his own Catalan origins for help. In so doing, Miró was following a trend toward using a kind of primitivism as inspiration in order to avoid traditional academic forms. Other artists had already discovered such sources as prehistoric and folk art or the art of children and the emotionally disturbed. However, Miró did not have to leave his world to find such raw and expressive qualities. Instead, he could turn inward – a natural thing for such a reserved artist.

Miró was, of course, not only a child of his middle-class parents, but also a child of turn-of-the-century Barcelona. At this time Spain had experienced a great change within its national consciousness, brought about by the country's defeat in the Spanish-American War, the destruction of its naval fleet and its loss of Cuba, Puerto Rico, the Philippines and Guam (1898). The liberal middle class had to concede that Spain was no longer a world power, moreover, it began to resent the corrupt government in Madrid, which manipulated the country's progressive constitution and elections towards its own ends. This dissent began to express itself within intellectual and cultural circles in a call for renewal, for example, in the resurrection of the idea that culturally independent areas like Catalonia or the Basque provinces should become independent states. This corroborated the anarchistic desire of Spanish workers and farmers for total self-determination, free of control from Madrid. Industrialization strengthened these currents, since it had brought about a new distribution of wealth in the south, where the natural resources had attracted mines and factories. However, cultural revitalization was a controversial subject. The national identity broke down into regional identities. These, in turn, had to be rooted in tradition, yet open to the developments and spirit of the twentieth century.

Portrait of V. Nubiola, 1917

Barcelona was a cosmopolitain city with an active cultural life, yet the visual arts were controlled there by official associations of painters – the powerful "Les Arts i les Artistes" group and the "Cercle Artístic de Barcelona". Miró needed to enter this community. In 1913, he joined the "Cercle Artístic de Sant Lluc" for drawing classes and for the opportunity of showing his work along with that of the other members. (The Sant Lluc group was a splinter group of the "Cercle Artístic" whose tone was set by high moral principles and Christian virtue.) The spirit of cultural renewal had formulated itself in the "Noucentisme" group, a conservative movement that thought that new Catalan art should be true to its Mediterranean heritage. The Noucentists posted the tenets of harmony, structure and measure, all of which, of course, are in themselves quite relative terms refering to classicism. The Noucentists accepted avant-garde artists very selectively: Cubism, for example, was seen as an attempt to reach a new ideal form in the classical sense. At the same time, Marcel Duchamp's Futurist-inspired *Nude descending a staircase* from 1912 was attacked for its "monstrosity" and anti-classicism[12], since it included the dimension of motion.

Although he deeply felt himself to be a Mediterranean artist, Miró was opposed to the selective judgement of the Noucentists. He felt that Catalan artists should remain as open as possible to impulses from abroad. Although he had never travelled beyond Catalonia – not even to Madrid – Miró became familiar with international developments in the arts. He read the poems, art criticism and articles in avant-garde Catalan and French magazines. His friends who travelled were careful to describe their impressions to him in eloquent letters. And there were also several exhibitions which offered a view of recent art, most importantly those shown by the gallerist Josep Dalmau, who had, for example, shown Cubist painters in 1912.

Miró's early work is caged in by his knowledge of contemporary art. Especially the Fauves influenced him, that group of expressive colourists who carried van Gogh's vision even further and whose most famous member was Henri Matisse. Miró used the accepted genres of still life, portrait and landscape to exercise his fledgling style. Sometimes, like in what is probably the earliest surviving oil painting by Miró, *The Farmer* (ill. p. 8), from 1914, the heavy brush-

Portrait of Heriberto Casany, also called: *The Chauffeur,* 1918
From 1917 to the beginning of 1918 Miró produced a series of portraits influenced by the Expressionists. The portraits of Nubiola and Casany show how Miró altered his technique in favour of the subject: whereas the highly rhythmised composition makes *Nubiola* seem restless, the *Chauffeur* seems to rest within itself due to its self-contained form.

Prades, the Village, 1917
The landscape is transformed into abstract patterns, whose lines, however, capture the strong impression of the natural model.

Miró and his friend Yvo Pascual in front of the silhouette of the village of Prades, 1917

Ciurana, the Path, 1917
Miró has put aside nature's palette and has largely done away with illusionistic space. The abstract contrasts seem to show him testing out colour constellations.

strokes lying clumsily next to one another tend to obscure the motif without having any saving graces of their own. The viewer can almost feel Miró struggling to coordinate the paint, his hand and his eye. A still life like *Wall Clock and Lantern* from 1915 is somewhat more successful. Here Miró emancipates some of the objects and shadows from their actual colours. Especially in the red cloth in the foreground, the paint dominates the subject of the work. The brush stroke, that is, the visible token of the painter's craft, bullies the small clock and lantern, the fruit and cloth that Miró has arranged picturesquely on the table top. These objects are taken from the household and have no voice of their own. Miró is so busy painting that he is not touched by the message of the traditional Vanitas symbols he has chosen to show.

In a letter from 1916 Miró writes, "We have a splendid winter ahead. Dalmau is showing the Simultaneists: Laurencin…, Gleizes, who wrote the book on Cubism together with Metzinger. The classic Impressionists and the modern

"I have turned inwards into myself, and the more sceptical I became about my surroundings, the closer I came to those places where the spirits live: the trees, the mountains, friendship."

17

'Fauves' will be at the French exhibition."[13] This French exhibition that Miró was so looking forward to was a major art event in Barcelona. It was a substitute for the large annual show of the important French painting societies, which, because of the First World War, could not take place in Paris. The catalogue had 1462 entries. Miró was not disappointed. It was his first face-to-face meeting with paintings by Renoir, Bonnard, Matisse, Monet, and Redon, among others. The war had swept some French artists and intellectuals over to neutral Spain as well. In Barcelona they often collected in Josep Dalmau's gallery, where, for example, in 1917 Miró met the Cuban Dadaist Francis Picabia, who had come to Barcelona to publish several issues of his influential avant-garde magazine "391".

In general, Catalan sentiment was pro-France during the war, which deflected not only artists, but also wealth to Spain. Miró, who did not enjoy being a soldier, could become quite virulent when speaking of the Germans: "These days of the successful allied offensive are for us Francophiles the greatest joy. We will see if they can throw out this uncouth mob once and for all, and then we will all go to Paris and surrender ourselves to France's delights, which we can see in their most expressive form in Renoir's painting (his *Moulin de la Galette*, his women, his nudes!)."[14] A negative attitude towards Germany and its culture was considered to be almost an open declaration of leftist intellectual sympathies during this period.[15] Around this time, Miró dared to show some of his work to the gallerist Dalmau, who promised him a solo exhibition in the gallery at the beginning of 1918. With this opportunity in his mind, Miró began to paint more canvases than he had ever painted before. The Fauves were still inspiring him. Not that Miró wanted to emulate French painting, or any existing work for that matter. Theoretically he considered all past styles, however recent, to be sand traps. How might one then explain Miró's dependence on modern French painting at this point? It was probably a form of rebellion. Despite loyalties to his homeland, Miró had difficulty accepting all of the conservative Catalan artists' demands, who seemed to be looking for a defined Catalan style as a flag around which to gather. He was young, but already quite sure of what he thought about modern developments in painting and he was not about to soften on his stance. Miró was too much of an individualist to simply subscribe to an aesthetic party platform of Mediterranean art, which wanted to move forward, but only at a safe trot. In a letter from 1917 to his friend and studio-mate Ricart, the twenty-four-year-old Miró wrote, "Here, in Barcelona, we lack courage. When the critics who are most interested in the modern and ultramodern movements find themselves in front of an outmoded academic, they melt and end up speaking well of him."[16]

Miró resolved to be uncompromising. His first one-man show at Dalmau's gallery ran for three weeks from January to February of 1918 and contained sixty-four canvases and many drawings dating from 1914 to 1917. Some of the work was damaged in the violent reaction to the images. Perhaps the *Portrait of E.C. Ricart* (ill. p. 13) from 1917 was among the paintings exhibited. It incorporated a Japanese print in the background with the glaring colours of the Fauves. The bold abstract patterning of Ricart's clothing almost crushes the delicate, flowing lines of the image behind him. His face is cartoon-like, but also suggestive of romanesque portraits in its frontality and linear stylization.

In a picture like *Ciurana, the Path* (ill. p. 17), 1917, painted in the hilly landscape near Montroig, Miró has put aside nature's palette. The individual brush-

Poster Design for the Magazine "L'Instant", 1919

strokes have integrated themselves into a rhythym of bright, broken colours that dip and rise in groupings of flat, striped patterning. Miró has almost done away with illusionistic space here. He seems to be testing out colour theories in his abstract contrasting of yellows and greens and blues and purples. Another work from 1917, *North-South* (ill. p. 19), a still life, reveals a bit of Miró's cultural and inspirational background. Arranged in a centrifuge of colour (a table top), there are hints of folk art, song, growth, collage and literature (maybe Goethe's colour theory). In the middle of the table lies the French poet Pierre Reverdy's brand new magazine "Nord-Sud", which was named after the Paris metro line connecting Montmartre with Montparnasse. "Nord-Sud" began its publication with a bow to Guillaume Apollinaire, the experimental, amusing and brilliant poet, critic and intellectual whom Miró read. With Tristan Tzara and André Breton as authors, the magazine opened the road to Dada and Surrealism. Though

North-South, 1917
This still life reveals something of the cultural influences on Miró. There are references to folk art and literature as well as to the French avant-garde, represented by the magazine "Nord-Sud" which pioneered Dada and Surrealism.

The Vegetable Garden with Donkey, 1918
These two pictures are rich in detail, reflecting Miró's treasuring of small things, of the "unimportant".

far away in Spain, which in 1917 was going through a violent political crisis, Miró had his finger on the pulse of an era.

Later in 1918, Miró and some of his like-minded friends finally ended up forming their own group within the Sant Lluc group which they named after the painter Gustave Courbet, whom they admired for his radicality. The "Courbet" group (Miró, E.C. Ricart, J.F. Ràfols, F. Domingo and R. Sala, later joined by Llorens Artigas) considered itself the progressive subset of the artists in Barcelona. It planned to "step over all the rotting bodies and fossils"[17] of the local art world and leave them behind. They exhibited in the rooms of the "Cercle Artístic de Sant Lluc". Their paintings were strident and colourful, definitely not the new classicism expected by dominant conservative artists. The Courbet group was not looking for approval and it did not get much. The predictable tone of rejection is reflected in the comment of one fellow painter who visited the first exhibition and exclaimed, "If this is painting, then I am Velázquez!"[18] From July to early December of 1918, Miró remained in Montroig. He must have been thinking about his first exhibitions and about the art world in Barcelona. Some of the harsh criticism might have struck him as partly true; at any rate, another stage of development began. Ràfols, a fellow member of the Courbet group who later wrote about Miró, called it his "detailistic phase". Jacques Dupin, Miró's biographer, called it "poetic realism". In July of 1918 Miró writes to Ricart, "I started working only a few days ago. – I have been at Montroig since the beginning of the month; the first week I was here I didn't want to think about dirtying a canvas or about anything at all. – In the morning to the beach to lie belly up and… in the afternoon an excursion or bicycling for kilometres. The second week I began thinking about working and in the middle of last week I started two landscapes. No simplifications or abstractions, my friend. Right now what interests me most is the calligraphy of a tree or a rooftop, leaf by leaf, twig by twig, blade of grass by blade of grass, tile by tile. This does not mean that these landscapes will not finally end up being Cubist or wildly synthetic. But we shall see… Next winter the gentlemen critics will continue to say that I persist in my disorientation."[19]

Miró was painting outside and meditating while doing it. He must have been reading the American poet Walt Whitman, particularly the "Song of Myself":

"I loaf and invite my soul, I lean and loaf at my ease observing a spear of summer grass." In the country, he seemed less concerned with the issue of painting style than in trying to show his beloved Montroig. He painted four land-

The Waggon Tracks, 1918
"The moment I begin to work on a canvas, I fall in love with it, the love that is the daughter of gradual understanding. A slow appreciation of the manifold nuances, the concentrated glory of the sun. It is a joy to await an understanding of a blade of grass in the countryside – why belittle it? This blade of grass that is equally as beautiful as a tree or a mountain."
Joan Miró

Ill. right:
Miró in his Paris studio in the Rue François Mouthon, 1931

Ill. below:
Self-Portrait, 1917

Ill. p.23:
Self-Portrait, 1919
This self-portrait was painted during Miró's first years in Paris. The folds and swells of his face appear chiselled, the gaze of the young man is fixed calmly on the observer. The portrait does not as much reveal as signalize his determination to go his own way as an artist in Paris.

scapes from around the farm: *The Vegetable Garden with Donkey* (ill. p. 20), *The Brick Factory, The House with the Palm Tree* and *The Waggon Tracks* (ill. p. 21). The landscapes share a naive treatment of details, combining the way things are counted out and included in gothic retables with delicate decorative patterning. His colours have changed, become more natural and earthen. Just a month later he wrote to J.F. Ràfols, "This week I hope to finish two landscapes... As you see, I work very slowly. As I work on a canvas I fall in love with it, love that is born of slow understanding. Slow understanding of the nuances – concentrated – which the sun gives. Joy at learning to understand a tiny blade of grass in a landscape. Why belittle it? – a blade of grass is as enchanting as a tree or a mountain. – Apart from the primitives and the Japanese, almost everyone overlooks this which is so divine. – Everyone looks for and paints only the huge masses of trees, of mountains, without hearing the music of blades of grass and little flowers and without paying attention to the tiny pebbles of a ravine – enchanting. I feel the need for great discipline more everyday – the only way to arrive at classicism – (that is what we should strive for – classicism in everything). I consider those who are not strong enough to work from nature to be sick spirits and I refuse to believe in them..."[20]

In 1919 Miró painted a puzzling image: a *Self-Portrait* (ill. p.23) in which he is wearing the same collarless red shirt that Vicente Nubiola has on in Miró's portrait of him (ill. p.14). On Miró it looks like silk pyjamas. It flaps open at the throat, exposing a sensual expanse of neck and a small, yet vital angle of chest hairs. Somehow, he appears almost undressed. In comparison with the loud *Portrait of E.C. Ricart* (ill. p.13) two years earlier, Miró has captured a soft, hushed atmosphere here. The dimples, folds and swells of his young face appear chiselled, his hair impeccably trimmed and combed into the semblance of an oiled cap.

Perhaps the most interesting aspect of the painting is the similarity between the shirt's treatment and the detailistic patterned landscapes. Miró seems to need to build an abstracting foundation from which the individual – here a face and in

the landscapes a building, a donkey or a farmer – may rise. While one side of the pyjama probably shows its original pattern, the other side has been allowed to flower into a Cubist-inspired balance of triangular depths and folds. As a shirt Miró has put on, it functions as a kind of symbol of the way he used the appearance of Cubistic style, namely as a contemporary cliché clothing the thing he chooses to paint. Never do these angular forms really seem to have grown out of the structure of the entire image, or to be at one with it. Miró did not execute many portraits, and this is, apart from a further self-portrait from 1917 (ill. p. 22), the only painting of him as a young man. It shows the Miró who arrived in Paris in 1920, twenty-seven years old and determined to grow beyond existing schools of Parisian painting. Maybe that is what Picasso thought, too, when he bought the picture that year after meeting Miró for the first time.

A strong contrast between supporting base and things shown is demonstrated by *The Table (Still Life with Rabbit)* of 1920. While the table and the space around it has been broken down into stylized angular shapes, the rabbit, fish, vegetables, grape leaves and chicken are quite realistically painted. Of the objects on the table, only the inanimate wine jug has been conquered by style. Strangely enough, the animals look alive still, although they are probably meant to be food.

The Table (Still Life with Rabbit), 1920
On the table ornamented in Cubist style lie naturalistically presented animals and objects. Unlike the Cubists, Miró does not incorporate the realistic elements into the geometrical structure of the picture. Thus the unbridgeable gap between the two worlds remains.

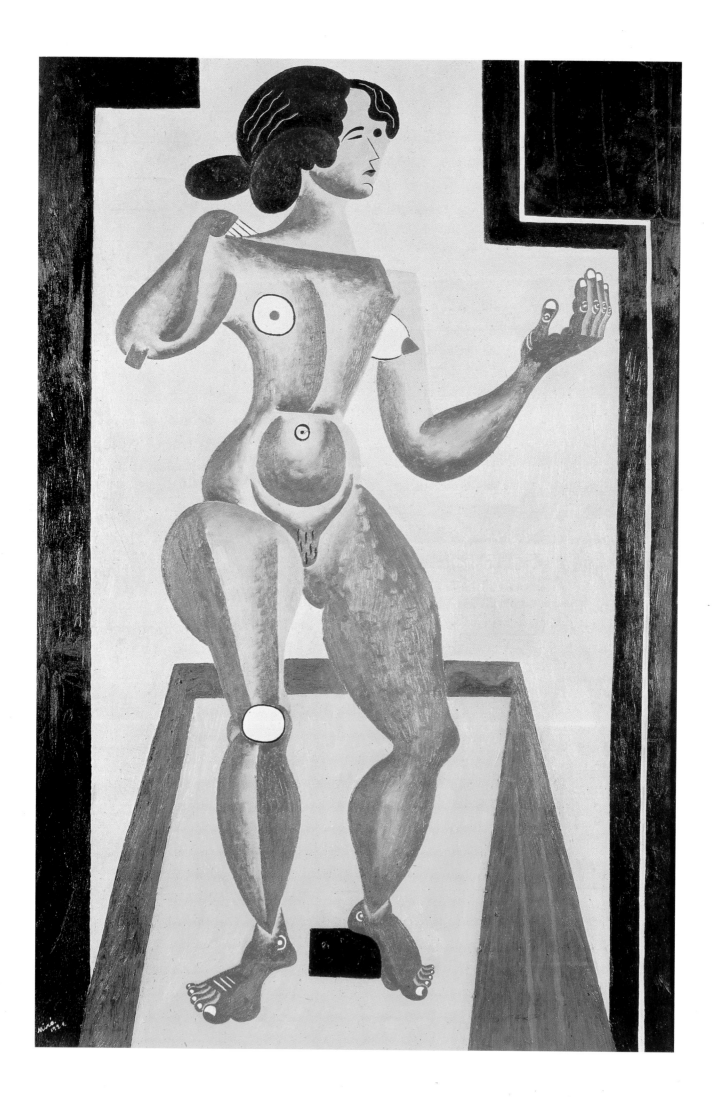

A Monk, a Soldier and a Poet

Miró arrived in Paris in 1920 after considerable preparation and careful consideration of just how he could finance his stay there. He wrote in one of his letters, "I, who currently have NOTHING, must earn my living whether it be here or in Paris or in Tokyo or in India", but he seems to have received a paltry sum from his mother to cover most expenses.[21] He lived in a hotel run by Catalans where many Catalan intellectuals stayed. Miró did not have a studio, which didn't matter since he was not able to paint. The city had simply overwhelmed him.

While Miró was in Paris, he met with Picasso, whose mother he had already visited in Barcelona to see her son's pictures there. Picasso was friendly towards him and supplied him with some introductions. "In the beginning Picasso – naturally-reserved with me – lately now, after having seen my work, very effusive; hours of conversation in his studio, very frequently…"[22] Dalmau arrived in Paris as well, and began making contacts for Miró. He actually managed to place some of Miró's paintings in private collections and showed his work to influential people.

Just about the same time Tristan Tzara came to Paris and started off Dada events in spring of 1920. Miró, who already knew several of the artists associated with Dada from Barcelona, kept up with these developments, even attending a Dada festival. Dada's poetic anarchy impressed Miró. Thus his experiences in Paris stimulated him in highly contradictory ways. At the same time that he was visiting the Louvre, that heaping treasure chest of art, Miró also exposed himself to a nihilistic group that propagated art's destruction as an institution. Miró wrote in 1920, "I much prefer the nonsense of Picabia or any one of the silly Dadaists to the easygoing ways of my compatriots in Paris, stealing from Renoir (whose only value now is as a classic) or producing a watered-down mixture of Sunyer and Matisse."[23] Miró seems to be echoing in his own way the message of Picabia's jokey work of 1920 in which he mounted a stuffed, dislocated monkey on a cardboard background and wrote in his own handwriting around the edges of the cardboard that it was a portrait of Cézanne, Rembrandt and Renoir.

After the initial wave of awe, Miró was able to recover his balance and observe the Paris art world with a critical eye. He recognized that a lot of contemporary painting was being done for sale and not as the necessary expression of some imminent idea. The idealist and moralist Miró, who had little money himself, became somewhat disgusted. In a letter that reveals his own high expectations of himself, as well as his religious reference point, he writes, "I have seen exhibitions of the moderns. The French are asleep. Rosenberg Exhibition. Works by Picasso and Charlot. Picasso very fine, very sensitive, a great painter. The visit to his studio made my spirits sink. Everything is done for his dealer, for the money. A visit to Picasso is like visiting a ballerina with a number of

Nude, 1917

Standing Nude, 1921
Miró increasingly makes use of basic geometric forms: fauvistic or cubistic leanings practically disappear, and the composition assumes greater importance. On one level, the picture shows a woman but it also shows a fitting together of working parts.

27

lovers… In other places I saw paintings by Marquet and Matisse; there are some that are very lovely, but they do a lot just for the sake of doing them, only for dealers and the money. In the galleries you see a lot of senseless junk… The new Catalan painting is infinitely superior to the French; I have absolute confidence that Catalan Art will be our saviour. When will Catalonia allow her pure artists to earn enough to eat and paint? Catalonia's rough way of treating spiritual things might be the Calvary of redemption. – The French (and Picasso) are doomed because they have an easy road and they paint to sell."[24] In July of 1920 he was back on the farm in Montroig, and began to work inspired by the jolts he had received in Paris. Still, it was the second trip to Paris that actually brought about a change in his work. In 1921 he managed to take over a Paris studio from the Spanish sculptor Pablo Gargallo, who taught in Barcelona during the winter months. The studio was in the Rue Blomet, and as fate would have it, it was right next door to where the artist André Masson had just rented a place for himself.

Miró's years spent in the Rue Blomet are treated by most historians as an heroic phase of his artistic career. Miró himself calls it "a decisive place, a decisive moment for me."[25] In his "Memories of the Rue Blomet", transcribed by Jacques Dupin, he gives a vivid picture of the time he spent there from 1921 to 1927. As Miró wrote, "More than anything else, the Rue Blomet was friendship, an exalted exchange and discovery of ideas among a marvellous group of friends."[26] The list of writers and artists that Miró got to know during these years reads like an intellectual history of the period, for example, Max Jacob, Michel Leiris, Roland Tual, Benjamin Péret, Pierre Reverdy, Paul Eluard, André Breton, Georges Limbour, Armand Salacrou, Antonin Artaud, Tristan Tzara, and Robert Desnos, but also Henry Miller, Ezra Pound and Ernest Hemingway. Particularly the poets of this group influenced Miró. They tried to get rid of structure and worn out imagery in exchange for immediate and brilliant sensory impressions. Often, their poetry was highly visual and object-oriented. Miró, who was reserved and kept to a rigorous work schedule with a soldier-like discipline, was drawn into this world through his proximity to the more gregarious André Masson. Masson could work with all kinds of visitors and activity around him, while Miró needed absolute solitude and peace and quiet.

In April of 1921, Miró had his first exhibition in Paris. It was at the gallery Licorne, which was known for its avantgarde shows. Not a single picture sold. Even for a man like Miró with a martyr-like attitude towards becoming an artist, this must have been a disappointment. In 1928, however, he was able to say, "that show wasn't talked about very much, but the few people who did talk about it had high hopes for me and were sure I'd end up being accepted."[27] When he returned to Montroig in the summer, he made a serious attempt to eliminate stylistic clichés from his work; fauvistic and cubistic leanings practically disappeared. However, a new influence makes itself felt – that of an art using basic geometric forms. Shortly before and during the First World War, Marcel Duchamp and Francis Picabia had began making images that showed fantastic "machines" with cogs, gears, pipes, screws and other undefined abstract parts. Often these machine parts had an anatomical, particularly a sexual intent. They were highly inventive, yet at the same time they illustrated the trend toward using abstract geometric forms that was spreading throughout Europe as Constructivism, De Stijl and Bauhaus. Miró followed the trend under Picabia's protection, thus keeping himself at a distance from the more political as-

Standing Nude, 1918

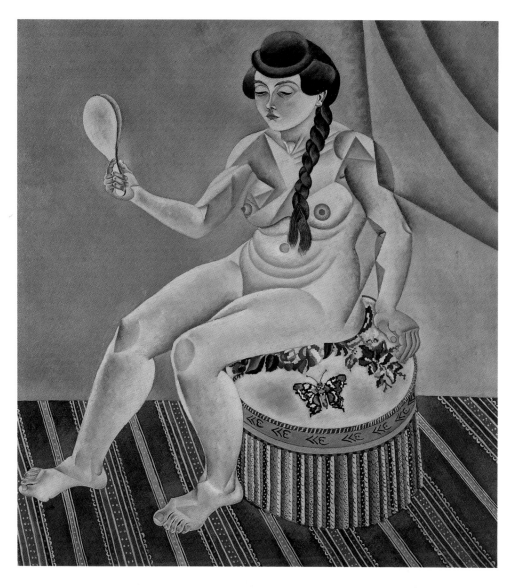

Nude with Mirror, 1919
Whereas the embroidery on the stool appears almost tangible, the square formality of the woman removes her from the observer: her body appears as a protective armour, her face expressive of a mysterious, inwardly directed calm.

pects of this development in form, which, in general, was associated with social reform. In a painting like *Standing Nude* from 1921 (ill. p. 26), Miró has placed the female figure upon a construct of parallelogram and rhombus, with her left foot resting upon a black rectangle. Behind her is a field of squared off blue, that has been set off by squared off bars of black – one of them interrupted by a white line that retraces its angular shape. Her breasts appear piercing and hard, like bullets. At the same time, her frozen gesture and the delineation of her anatomy has a Romanesque quality, such as in the circular knee cap and the partitioning of her body. Instead of the repetitive beating of pattern encountered in his landscapes, Miró sets out here to create a counter-point rhythm. The zigzagging movement from the black block under the model's foot, to her white knee cap, pubic hairs, the white breasts and fingernails and the model's black hair pull the viewer's eyes back and forth up the canvas. The white border line to the right lights up the side of the canvas to which the model is looking. The black square area facing her echoes the square beneath her foot. All in all, the composition, which is relatively empty and flat, appears highly constructed. On one level, the picture shows a woman, but it also shows a fitting together of working parts. Here Miró demonstrates a repeated use of abstract geometric shapes that actively point toward the balance of forms. From now on, balance was to become a presence, not only a compositional element in Miró's work.

Sitting Nude, 1917/18

The Farm, 1921/22
A key work of Joan Miró, this picture is open to numerous interpretations. The author Ernest Hemingway bought the picture because he saw his impressions of the Catalan landscape and mentality reflected in it.

Miró's most famous painting and a so-called "key" to his work, *The Farm* (ill. p. 30) was also begun in 1921. It, too, contains numerous abstract elements and correspondences that would be hard to explain without the new influence, for example, the black circle and the white base of the eucalyptus tree in the middle of the painting, the red square to its right defying the depth of the chicken coop it describes, the red tiles and rhomboid section of black to the lower left, and even the round moon (could the sun be that pale?), the red wagon wheel and the rooster's perch. The lyric softness and organic forms of Miró's previous landscapes are gone. He has chosen to show many metal and wooden objects, which do not overlap each other and stand out in their hard-edged entirety against the background. The hard thorniness of the standing nude woman (ill. p. 26) is echoed here in the spiny trunk of the nearly leafless Eucalyptus tree and the stony, dry, red-brown earth.

In *The Farm*, Miró uses some aspects of Romanesque style. For example, the size of various details does not accord with nature and perspective, but rather with Miró's feeling about their importance. He writes, "I don't think it makes sense to give more importance to a mountain than an ant (but landscape artists just can't see that)…"[28]

While the Romanesque artist was constructing the hierarchy of animals and people in his compositions, he was acutely aware that he must control their isolated strength by binding them tightly into the composition through a tension of balance and symmetry. It was a highly conscious form of art comparable to architecture, not so much interested in telling a story or showing reality than in erecting a conceptual framework for a Christian mind-set.

Miró was having a difficult time melding contemporary and traditional factors, particularly since he wanted to avoid style. "During the nine months I worked on *The Farm* I was working seven or eight hours a day. I suffered terribly, horribly, like a condemned man. I wiped out a lot and I started getting rid of all those foreign influences and getting in touch with Catalonia."[29]

The farm in Montroig was the source of life energy for Miró: "…The Earth of Montroig: I can actually feel it, and more and more; but even as a small boy I felt it. For me it was a physical need."

In the main axis of *The Farm*, the story appears to be one of fertility – possibly as a metaphor of artistic productivity – with related details strewn about the surface of the painting like upon a medieval tapestry. It is intriguing to "read" the repetitive references. Right in the foreground Miró has placed a red-spouted watering can for whom a bucket has tipped its skirt. Behind it is a French newspaper whose name "L'Intransigeant" (The Uncompromising) is truncated by a fold so that only the syllable meaning "into" or "within" remains. Referring as it does to the watering can under which it has been placed, it seems to be a written instruction to the male moistener. If we follow the tiles and small path to the back, we see seven imprints of bare feet that stop suddenly without having got any further. The path, however, continues along to a square well or water trough. A woman is leaning over it and there are a few pots, a bucket and a bottle near her. Behind her, and positioned almost in the middle of the painting like its perspective point, is a squatting, idol-like figure, hairless and naked, foetal and frog-like, with extreme shadowing on one half of its body.

Is it her child? Is the dog barking at it or at the moon, like on a later painting of Miró (cf. ill. p. 47)? Behind the well is a pump or mill that is powered by a mule harnessed into a circular tract, going around and around and not getting anywhere, but still accomplishing something. The rooster, the rabbits and the goat add sexual aspects, but they are also details of life on the farm at Montroig. The vegetation is sparse; either the crops are somewhere else or the farm, unkempt as it appears, is no longer in working order. On the lower left a huge wild plant erupts into bloom. It may well be the large type of algarve cactus that flowers only once every seven years in a cycle of slow but dramatic fertility. Considering Miró's struggling development, these details might hint that he finally felt himself approaching the right source.

The Farm is dominated by the light, framing buildings of chicken coop and stall, and the eucalyptus tree in the centre. In one sense it is a highly architectural painting, because it is so carefully constructed. Miró reworked the painting many times, bringing it with him to Barcelona and Paris. He always stressed the difficulty of completing it. As he told in an interview late in his life, expanding the time he worked on it, "It took me practically two years to finish it, but not because I had any trouble actually painting it. No, the reason it took so long was that what I saw underwent a metamorphosis. The painting was absolutely realistic. I didn't invent anything. I only eliminated the fencing on the front of the chicken coop because it kept you from seeing the animals. Before this metamorphosis occurred I had to capture even the smallest detail of that farm I had right there before my eyes in Montroig. For instance, I very carefully copied that big eucalyptus tree in the center of the canvas. Every time I strayed from the model, I'd take one of those pieces of blackboard chalk that schoolchildren use and I'd chalk over what I'd done and make the necessary corrections. I was thoroughly convinced that I was working on something very important, attempting to summarize the world around me."[30]

Table with Glove, 1921

The tree, with its deep roots and potential for growth, were a literary symbol of the Catalan people[31], which may be why Miró put a eucalyptus in the centre of the farm. The Barcelona architect Antoni Gaudí, a fellow Catalan much admired by Miró, also once explained the tree as his inspirational source. Gaudí, who died in 1926 after being hit by a streetcar, once pointed to the eucalyptus tree outside his window and said, "An upright tree; it carries its branches and these carry the twigs, which in turn carry the leaves. And every single part grows harmoniously, magnificent, since the artist God himself has made it. This tree doesn't need any exterior help. All parts are balanced in themselves."[32] Although Gaudí and Miró refer to two different eucalyptus trees, they are both metaphoric images of a natural and national correctness of expression and functionality. Usually a comparison is made between the undulating lines of Miró's later work and the curving lines of Gaudí's architecture, thus marking the Art Nouveau origins of Miró's line. There might, however, be parallels to be found in less obvious ways, such as in the methods of working and in both men's dedication to re-inventing Catalan art within both Catalan tradition and the context of the twentieth century. Gaudí, for example erected most of his main works in brick or stone instead of using more modern materials. Yet he was mainly concerned with the functional form as it grew from structure. Gaudí's unconventional architectural solutions to the problem of dealing with weights and supports may have directly influenced Miró.

There is at least one more strain of contemporary influence hovering within

The Farm (ill. p.30), that is, that of the naive. By 1921 when Miró painted his key work, naive painting had been recognized by the avantgarde art world as a genre in its own right. Henri Rousseau had established a laboured realism that inadvertently underbid conventional expectations of art and appeared humorous, enigmatic or dispossessed. Rousseau, the home-grown primitive, was loved and feted by the avantgarde; his work was wrong at the right time. Just as Rousseau placed his figures into a set-like situation, similar to the way a child would place a doll into a doll house or a photographer would pose his subjects before a studio landscape, so, too, did Miró lift and place the objects into his composition. However, while Rousseau created a frozen stillness within his images, Miró managed to breathe life to the things he showed in *The Farm*. In this way Miró, who spent much of his childhood in the Catalan countryside, was perhaps more truly child-like than Rousseau. As anyone knows who has experienced very small children, nothing, not even a two-dimensional image, is inanimate to them. Miró never fully explained the meaning of *The Farm*, but insisted that it was merely Montroig for him. (He did, however admit to altering the wall of the

The Carbide Lamp, 1922/23
In this picture Miró drastically reduces the objects to clearly delineated forms arranged against a flat background. While the lamp is slightly shaded, the fruit and grid are composed of lines only.

stable by adding moss and cracks so that the patterned surface look more in balance with the chicken coop wire.)[33] After it was rejected by many galleries, Ernest Hemingway bought the picture. He had to scrape the money together to do so, and later he gave the painting to his wife, who lent it to the National Gallery of Art in Washington, where it can be seen today. Hemingway repeats Miró's claim that he painted it in nine months[34], "as much time it takes for a woman to make a baby" – a statement that intuitively picks up on the intimations of fertility and gestation in the painting. Miró's relationship to the farm was, however familiar, still that of an urban bourgeois visitor who preserved his mental distance from real farm life. As late as 1930, over 49 per cent of the working population in Spain were still farmers. During the Second World War, even more people worked the land from necessity. At that point, Miró himself would also consider the farm in Montroig as a possible source of income. In his Catalan Notebooks of 1940–1941 he writes about trying to reorganize his life to become financially independent so that he might remain a true poet, "and never let my-

The Farmer's Wife, 1922/23
Miró explains the circle next to the cat as an afterthought: "I found that during the first stages of painting the farmer's wife I had made the cat too big and this disrupted the picture's balance. That is the reason for the double circles and the two angular lines in the foreground. They look symbolic, esoteric; yet they have no fantasy character."

The Ear of Corn, 1922/23
Like *The Carbide Lamp, The Ear of Corn* is a very reduced picture. It reflects Miró's formal interset in linear shapes as demonstrated in the grains.

self go so far as to become a businessman… must go into the matter of the farmhouse seriously, it would afford me an independent livelihood and, what's more, this direct contact with the soil and the men who till it and the elements involved in it would be of great human value to me, they would enrich me as a man and as an artist."[35] In a way, Miró was a true Romantic, using the authenticity of the farmers and landscape as a raw material that he focused on. Perhaps he succeeded in capturing the essence of the farm for himself, while at the same time giving expression to all of the art world impulses weighing on his mind.

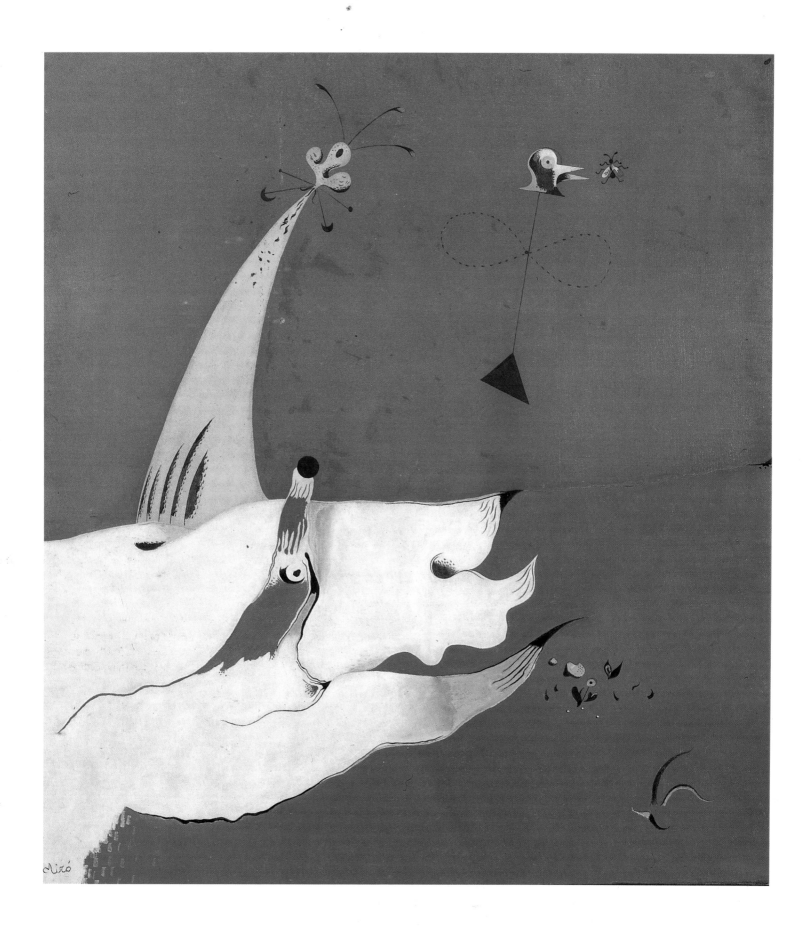

Poetic License

A change had been building up in Miró's work. From 1923 he began to invent a new cosmos of beings and symbols. In *The Tilled Field* (ill. p. 38) it is possible to still identify the farm at Montroig. Yet, the animals, house, fields and plants have become disquieting presences, stretched, swollen and barbed sometimes even into ugliness. At the same time, they insist on their identities. Miró appears to be giving an anti-cerebral, pro-sensual message in the painting. A large lizard with a dunce cap becomes a jack-in-the-box that pops out of a pipe in a startling greeting. The fish, only head, has lost its body, suggesting a stinky smell and the proximity to sea. The ear is a giant listener. The eye in the crown of the tree sees all. Barbs invite and dispel touch. Miró is showing how he loves his Catalan homeland with his body and its senses, yet the landscape seems ultimately to resist him. It awakens his reverence, but it is not paradise. The flags waving on the gnarled tree – Catalan, Spanish and French – tip up in optimistic crescents. Birds wheel in the sky next to a cactus-tree's triangular crown. Freedom? The folded newspaper in the foreground says "Day" to us in French, but a little night is falling diagonally onto the upper right corner of the painting, where something is hanging – a large spider or perhaps only a leaf.

In its startling juxtaposition of figures, *The Tilled Field* owes something to the collage; in its subject matter to contemporary poetry and writing. For example, Margit Rowell and Rosalind Krauss identified the lizard in the foreground as "Merlin the wizard, fitted with his traditional conic hat", from Apollinaire's "The Decaying Magician".[36] Of course, since Miró spent a lot of his time reading between bouts of painting, it is not surprising for him to continue an imaginary dialogue with the authors he read in his work. Just as the flag forms a bridge to a cactus, so too, do the books he has brought to Montroig form an intellectual bridge back to Paris.

At any rate, Miró's reading was not a relaxing activity. "In the room that serves as my studio I always have books, and I read during the breaks in my work. This demands a constant spiritual vibration from me."[37] It may well be that versions of particular characters and images from this reading matter often found themselves into Miró s paintings, however never in the form of an illustration. Rather, such characters were actually present in Montroig because Miró projected them into the landscape with his thoughts. We know, too, that in a reverse process, Miró brought small objects like toys, ceramic whistles, grass, small flags, and shells with him from Spain back to Paris. Miró was constantly sifting and sorting his real and imaginary acquaintances and worlds according to their possibilities of meaning and effect.

The Hunter (ill. p. 39) of 1923/24 is almost the same size as *The Tilled Field* (ill. p. 38), and it has some similarities in its placement of forms. The subject matter that belongs to these forms, however, has been somewhat changed. Obviously, even more of recognizable reality has been left behind. The abstract cir-

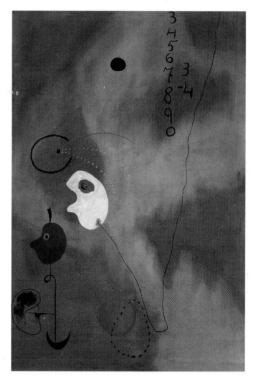

The Calculation, 1925
In the twenties, a period of great importance for Miró, he produced the so-called "picture poems", in which the artist combined colours and words or numbers.

Landscape, 1924/25
Figures from a new and mythical world appear in Miró's early and meticulous method of painting. The small and unprepossessing stand in the centre: the ear of corn and the flower become as large as trees, and the insects take on the role of people.

The Tilled Field, 1923/24

In the years 1923/24 Miró finds a new language of imagery which translates the observation of nature and the magical value of objects into a system of signs and colours. The transition can be seen in **The Tilled Field**: the objects have not quite been transformed into an independent world of signs.

cular base of the tree in *The Farm* (ill. p. 30) has developed itself into the symbol for a tree – here as a large, light and slightly irregular circle marked by a black point, a diagonal line and a single leaf. It corresponds to the Carob tree in *The Tilled Field* on the right side of the painting, and also has an eye growing out of it. To the left, a stick figure resembling the cactus-like tree in *The Tilled Field* indicates a human figure: the hunter. He is wearing the traditional Catalan hat on his head and smoking a pipe. Several small tongues of flame which issue from his pipe and his rifle, as well as the flame next to his yearning heart give him a passionate aura. The conical rifle that the hunter holds in the middle of the painting corresponds to the chimney of the house in *The Tilled Field*. The spider/leaf object seems to re-occur as a sun-egg in *The Hunter*. The fish is larger but still somehow missing its fleshy body. It is made up of a head with tongue, whiskers, an ear and eye, a bowel, a genital and a tail. These parts of its anatomy are connected by a straight line, much as are the remaining cones, triangles and circles of the rest of the composition. Once it is recognized as a sardine, however, its parts seem to be more cohesive. In fact, the whole painting begins to change when the characters are logically identified: centres form that are less a result of the composition than of the viewer's understanding of it. As a comparison of *The Tilled Field* and *The Hunter* demonstrates, Miró repeats and orders forms while changing some of their meanings. Yet above and beyond any anecdotal understanding is Miró's formal development. He has progressed even further in the direction of Picabia and Duchamp's machine art. "Less is more" was the credo of a whole generation of artists and architects aiming for clarity and impact. Miró follows this trend and empties out *The Hunter*, leaving only the most speaking of details. Again, he is looking for balance and a working together of parts. Because the parts float so freely against their background, "The Hunter" almost looks like one of the mobiles that Miró's friend, Alexander Calder, would construct several years later.

The background of Miró's paintings has become thin and transparent or smooth and opaque. It has abandoned its attempt to show real space or real things and has borrowed the qualities of nature herself. How can one show the brightness of sunlight streaming through a blue sky and reflecting from waves? By making the sky and sea a glowing, warm yellow. In a similar way, the ground has been thinly washed or rubbed with ochre and red, which become pastel tones through their thinness. Because the upper and lower halves of *The Hunter* and *The Tilled Field* are so close to each other in colour and intensity, the canvas hardly appears divided into heaven and earth. Light is flooding and flattening the landscape, against which single forms may stand out. Particularly *The Hunter* has become flat, easily comparable to the pages of a book. Miró has finally reached what he was looking for in 1920 when he wrote, "I am working hard; going toward an art of concept, using reality as a point of departure, never as a stopping place."[38]

Study for: *Catalan Landscape,* 1923/24

Catalan Landscape (The Hunter), 1923/24
The world of objects has been reduced to a few signs. Only the pipe of the hunter can be recognized, everything else is reduced to a few lines.

"How did I think up my drawings and my ideas for paintings? Well I'd come home to my Paris studio in the Rue Blomet at night, I'd go to bed, and sometimes I hadn't any supper. I saw things, and I jotted them down in a notebook. I saw shapes on the ceiling…"

Harlequin's Carnival, 1924/25
The Surrealist championing of the sub-conscious begins to influence Miró. Remembered dreams become a source of inspiration in these small paintings.

These studies clearly illustrate that Miró's pictures do not arise spontaneously despite associative and coincidental elements. The compositional plan for the ***Harlequin's Carnival*** is proof of careful planning, whereas the study for ***Siesta*** is already an exact preformulated version of the painting.

In 1924, the year André Breton published the first Surrealist Manifesto, Miró made several more paintings in this vein. A relatively small canvas, *Harlequin's Carnival*, 1924/25 (ill. pp. 40/41), which Miró himself "illustrated" with a poetic text published in 1939 in the magazine "verve", brought this phase to a climax. It continues the all-over distribution of weights and counter-weights in the form of amusing invented creatures celebrating an indoor carnival. A mechanical guitarist plays the music, while the others play games. The characters are beginning to look familiar: an insect jack-in-the-box has popped up out of a trunk, a fish lies on the table, a ladder, flames, stars, leaves, cones, circles, spheres and lines appear. Particularly the ladder has gained in importance since its introduction in the chicken coop of *The Farm* (ill. p. 30). It offers Miró a good opportunity of using connecting straight diagonal lines, while at the same time lending itself to poetic meanings. There is one detail of the carnival painting that does not seem "fantastical" or "imaginative", as Miró's paintings are usually called. The mildew and cracks on the walls under and around the window are shown as stains and decay. Of course, Miró was aware of Leonardo da Vinci's famous advice to use chance wall markings, marble striations, shadows or clouds as the beginning of an image, and he has begun to pay attention to just such forms here. Such inspiration was being discussed in the artistic circles around Miró.

Chance markings could be developed into things. Eventually, Miró would establish an irregular ground of colour on his canvases and then look at the empty, flat, perhaps slightly transparent space and begin to people it with what the ground suggested to him. This also explains why the mildewed walls are explicitly included in *Harlequin's Carnival*. They represent one of the painter's starting points, an important source of inspiration that helped him to invent whole studios full of figures. Already the shapes on the wall next to the musical notes in the upper centre of the painting have taken on the shape of leaves, vines and flames. But this does not mean that the paintings developed spontaneously. Preliminary drawings exist for Miró's paintings, and they often include written mentions of colours, the format of the finished canvases and their titles. Around 1924, the drawings were squared and transferred grid for grid onto the larger canvas. (Today, a painter would use a slide or overhead projector.) Despite all of his romantic fantasy, Miró was a careful and meticulous planner. His pictures existed in a preliminary form in his mind and on paper long before they hit the canvas.

Miró once wrote, "How did I think up my drawings and my ideas for paintings? Well I'd come home to my Paris studio in Rue Blomet at night, I'd go to bed, and sometimes I hadn't any supper. I saw things, and I jotted them down in a notebook. I saw shapes on the ceiling..."[39]

Hungry in bed: unrestful sleep with remembered dreams – the Surrealist championing of the sub-conscious also began to influence Miró. He often mentioned working from hallucinations caused by hunger, which shows how little money he had for food, even though he always seemed to have enough money

"I am working hard; going toward an art of concept, using reality as a point of departure, never as a stopping place."
Joan Miró

43

Bathing Woman, 1925
In this picture, whose blue background is reminiscent of seascapes, the line takes on an important function: it no longer delineates, surrounding frozen forms – it has itself become movement leading the eye of the observer through the picture.

for soap, shoe polish, paint and trips back and forth to Spain. His poverty was probably not entirely unwelcome in this respect, since the circle of intellectuals and artists he was in daily contact with were practising all kinds of extremes to reach the primal voice they pictured deep inside of themselves. Compared to the use of ether, cocaine, alcohol, morphium, or sex, Miró's hunger-hallucinations look almost like a monkish fasting. He was too deeply spiritual to destroy his own body, the vessel of that spirit. As the constant references to sensual and sexual organs in his paintings suggest, he fully enjoyed his own connection with nature.

In a letter from Montroig he wrote, "During my off-hours I lead a primitive existence. More or less naked, I do exercises, run like a madman out in the sun, and jump rope. In the evening, after I've finished my work, I swim in the sea. I am convinced that a strong and healthy œuvre requires a healthy, vigorous body. I see no one here, and my chastity is absolute."[40]

In the fall of 1924, Miró met André Breton, Paul Eluard and Louis Aragon through his neighbour André Masson. The First Surrealist Manifesto was published in November. The following definition was contained in the lengthy Manifesto: "Surrealism, noun, masculine. Pure psychic automatism, by which one intends to express verbally, in writing or by any other method, the real functioning of the mind. Dictation by thought, in the absence of any control exercised by reason, and beyond any aesthetic or moral preoccupation.

Encycl. Philos. Surrealism is based on the belief in the superior reality of certain forms of association heretofore neglected, in the omnipotence of dreams, in the undirected play of thought…"[41]

On one level, Surrealism (the word was first used by Apollinaire in a theatre-programme text and as a subtitle in 1917) was a reaction against the unemotional, geometrical tendencies of art that began to win out in the twenties. Although explicitly a literary movement, the visual arts were mentioned in a footnote of the manifesto. Among the artists named were Paul Klee, Giorgio de Chirico, Marcel Duchamp, Francis Picabia, Man Ray, André Masson, and Max Ernst, as well as the "classics" Pablo Picasso, Henri Matisse, and Georges Seurat. Despite his exclusion of "aesthetic preoccupations" – by which he might have meant conventional beauty–, André Breton did not intend to exclude painters, who were simply another hinge to expression. Miró and Masson were very probably the first painters to make the jump into free association, with Max Ernst following closely behind.

While the subject matter of *The Tilled Field* (ill. p. 38) and *The Hunter* (ill. p. 39) were already dream-like, influenced by the sub-conscious, they remained tightly constructed-looking images that had both taken the better part of a year to complete.

In the summer of 1925, however, Miró created a work that seemed almost uncontrolled within the short space of just a few days. *The Birth of the World* had a murky background resembling a streaky, steamed window, against which Miró had set a few sharply defined forms in black, white and the primary colours. The title, invented by one of the Surrealist poets, refers to the process of genesis itself, and here the recognizability of that process is important. Whatever those things are that creation may have created, the painting quickly attained fame

Photo – that is the Colour of my Dreams,
1925
Confrontation with Surrealist poets in the years after 1924 played an important role in Miró's creative life. Words and sentences begin to people his canvases: an attempt to transcend painting and, at the same time, link it with poetry.

Person Throwing a Stone at a Bird, 1926
Lines continue to take up the narrative: a fantasy figure throws a stone at a rooster. Lines suggest the arm's momentum, the path of the stone and the rooster's flight, they direct the readability of the picture.

within the circle of insiders who saw it in Miró's studio, including Breton, who later likened its impact on artists to Picasso's *Demoiselles d'Avignon*. The painting's huge size magnified its unconventional stance; the new method of applying paint had inevitably led to a larger format, and *The Birth of the World* (about six by eight feet) was Miró's largest picture to date.

In *The Birth of the World*, Miró began by artificially creating the possibility of Surrealist "automatic" stimulus on the painting ground. He smeared the canvas irregularly with glue sizing. Layers of transparent bister and black glazes were poured and rubbed around, taking to the sizing with varying intensities. Then ochre glaze was allowed to drip down from the top, forming little rivulets. Miró also shook a brush dipped in ochre at the canvas to achieve sprays of little spots. The triangular form with a tail was developed from a large black area that seemed to Miró to need to be structured. (Miró: "It might be a bird"). A red accent, the blue lines, the little man were added one after another.[42] Automatic drawing and painting – letting the pencil or brush wander over a pictorial ground without a goal in mind – helped Miró find his motifs without looking for them. This relaxed the hold of the artist on his composition somewhat, even though he obviously still influenced it to a certain extent through his individual psychology. Yet as a comparison of *The Hunter* and *The Birth of the World* show, inspiration from the void brought about an entirely different kind of picture. It was a way of escaping one's own feeling for form by using chance spills, spots and shadings as a starting point. Any accidental form was a potential image. Of course, the accidental nature of the image's beginning were also a desired look.

Another work from 1925 remained almost completely empty. The indistinct blue background of *Painting* is relieved only by a tiny white circle in the upper left corner, and the artist's signature in the lower right corner. The poet Michel Leiris once wrote a long text about Miró's work in 1929, which calls up the spiritual and intellectual atmosphere of the period. It suggests a Buddhistic understanding of the world's entirety, which then focuses in on an extremely small and expressive detail of it. Obviously such an empty picture as the blue *Painting* from 1925 creates a space for meditation, but it needs a decisively set

Dog Barking at the Moon, 1926
The landscapes painted in 1926 show Miró as a colourist; both colours of the background are deep, forming an effective contrast for the primary colours red, yellow, and blue.

Jean Arp
Stable Head, 1926
Jean Arp had a lasting influence on Miró's
work. His undulating organic forms were
soon to become the idiom of the whole epoch.

Joan Miró (2nd from left) and Jean Arp
(sitting), 1927

to convince the viewer that it has honed a sensual encounter to its sharpest
point. In a letter to Leiris from 1924, Miró writes that the Japanese artist Hokusai "wanted to make a line or a dot perceptible, that's all"[43].

Clearly, Miró wants to create an effect in his painting similar to that of the
terse Japanese poetry form of haiku, which concentrates on fresh and momentary perception. In the same letter to Leiris as above, Miró includes the phrase,
"The eloquence of a cry of admiration made by a child in front of a blossoming
flower." Between the years 1925 and 1927 – his last years in the Rue Blomet –
Miró completed over one hundred and thirty pictures. (In the ten years before
this, he had only executed a total of about one hundred pictures in all.) Most of
the paintings were left untitled. The few titles Miró did allow were either invented by his poet friends after seeing the painting or were later derived from
the phrases Miró actually painted onto his canvases, much as Picabia did. *Musique, Seine, Michel, Bataille, et moi* from 1927, refers somehow to walks along
the bank of the Seine with Michel Leiris and Georges Bataille, whose interest in
the body's openings was shared by Miró. Another work and one of Miró's most
poetic, *Photo – that is the Colour of my Dreams*, 1925 (ill p. 45), also includes
words, which have been carefully written in an effeminate calligraphy. Here
Miró contrasts what the modern medium of photography and the traditional medium of painting can accomplish.

As time progresses, Miró's pictures become increasingly abstract, and his
forms more organic. Often the images of this period appear haunted by the spirit
of Paul Klee or Wassily Kandinsky. (Miró got to know Klee's work from a
small gallery in Paris in 1925.) Groups of formally related works often came
into being all at the same time, instead of being finished separately one after another. Despite the abstraction, it is often possible to recognize the traditional
genres of landscape, still life or portrait painting within the images. Dotted,
solid, curving and straight lines – and any combination thereof – play an important part in the balance of the paintings. The lines punctuate the pictures and direct their readability. In *Person Throwing a Stone at a Bird*, 1926 (ill. p. 46),
they suggest the arm's momentum, the path of the stone and the rooster's fright,
while also establishing a roughly triangular composition. The lines also are in
keeping with the flat picture plane in Miró's paintings, which share many of the
reductive aspects of printed comics. For example, *Landscape* (ill. p. 49), executed in Montroig in the summer of 1927, shows a humorous narrative situation expressed through highly simplified means.

In 1927, Miró left the Rue Blomet and moved to a studio near Jean Arp, Max
Ernst, Paul Eluard and René Magritte. Particularly Arp influenced Miró with the
undulating silhouettes of his figures. Softened, organic forms became the contemporary idiom as opposed to the more geometric and angular vocabulary of
Cubism's followers. Examples of these shapes are the rabbit (not duck) and balloon-like "flower" of *Landscape*, 1927. Such forms, whether defined by outlining or solid fields of colour, were to accompany Miró for the rest of his artistic
career. One year later, when Miró began to "redo" old master paintings, he used
his own colour schemes and biomorphic forms that sometimes resemble Arp's.

In 1928, the thirty-five-year-old Miró, who had seen very little of the world
up until that point, took a two-week trip to Belgium and Holland. He re-created
several Dutch anecdotal paintings and portraits, which appear schematized and
exaggerated like comic characters. Miró admired Dutch painting and did not intend to mock it. (One of Miró's free-floating comments was "The spiral stair-

case in 'The Philosopher' by Rembrandt")[44]. Instead, Miró adapted the seven-
teenth century work to contemporary subjective reflection. Obviously, such a
contrast of past and present styles agressively showed that painting had changed
entirely and that certain things were no longer possible. On the other hand, Miró
was certainly attracted to the symbolic details of Netherlandish painting, since it
must have reminded him of the anecdotal and poetically symbolic character of
his own work.

Miró painted his "old master" paintings in his studio, using picture postcards
from museum shops as a point of departure for his own versions of them, much
as Pop artists would do. But Miró was also capable of using other printed
material as a starting point. In a painting of 1929, he chose a Spanish advertisement for a German diesel motor to create *Queen Louisa of Prussia*[45] (ill. p.52),
as well as a reproduction of an additional unspecified image.

Miró saved the copy of advertisement, upon which he wrote, "Pour la Reine".
The general shape of the motor resembled an upright female figure with
protuberant breasts, a long skirt and a very small head. She has been placed
upon a canvas vibrant with contrasting colours arranged in an exceedingly spare
and unusually spatial situation. There is probably an explanation for this. The
"Queen" complements the emptiness of room with her body in almost exactly
the same way as did Georg Kolbe's realistic female nude statue in Mies van der
Rohe's Barcelona Pavilion of the same year. (Miró was visiting Barcelona in
February and September of 1929.) The composition of Miró's painting bears a

Landscape (The Hare), 1927
In 1927 Miró moved into a studio near Jean
Arp, Max Ernst, Paul Eluard, and René Magritte. Particularly Arp influenced Miró with
his undulating silhouettes and the organic
forms of his figures. The hare in this picture is
one example of this influence.

Dutch Interior I, 1928

Hendrick Martensz Sorgh
The Lutanist, 1661

During a trip to the Netherlands, Miró visited the museums in Amsterdam where he particularly admired the old masters of the 17th century. In these genre pictures he finds that same love of exactly formulated detail which had occupied him. He bought a series of picture postcards of these paintings, which he took to Paris with him and used as a starting point for the series of *Dutch Interiors* of 1928. In the pictures *Interior I* and *II* shown here, Miró made use of Hendrick Martensz Sorgh's *The Lutanist* as well as Jan Steen's *Cat's Dancing Lesson*. At first sight, these pictures have little in common with the 17th century paintings. A closer look shows, however, that each form of the *Dutch Interior* refers to part of the original painting. Miró attempted an exact transformation of all the details into the realm of the fantastic, as the series of preparatory sketches illustrates: each element, the scene,

and each person is retained. The process of transformation, however, also meant an exaggerated reduction or enlargement of parts of the composition. For instance, in *Dutch Interior II* the windows and chairs are reduced, while the head of the figure on the left is five times bigger than its body; colour, too, has asserted itself against the original.

Dutch Interior I and *II* present a re-creation of the old masters in a modern language of form and colour. In this way, Miró clearly illustrates what is possible in painting and present – as well as what is no longer possible.

Jan Steen
Cat's Dancing Lesson

Studies for:
Dutch Interior II, 1928

Queen Louisa of Prussia, 1929
A Spanish advertisement for a German diesel
motor was the starting point for this picture.

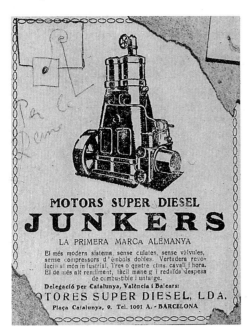

Sketch by Miró on an Advertisement, 1929

close resemblance to that of the most well-known photograph of the Kolbe
sculpture poised above the water surface in the courtyard of Mies's building.
Even the circular arm movement of Kolbe's figure seems to repeat itself in the
breast-like bulges of the queen. In a kind of blind intuition, Miró lighted upon
the image of the epoch that allied opposites: the temple of abstract International
Style architecture that Hitler would declare to be degenerate with the type of realistic sculpture that the Nazis supported. Although the original shape of the die-

Studies for:
Queen Louisa of Prussia, 1929

Portrait of Mrs Mills in 1750 (after Constable), 1929
This portrait is one of a series of "imaginary portraits" done according to historical portraits. As with the *Dutch Interiors*, Miró transforms them into his own, fantastic form language.

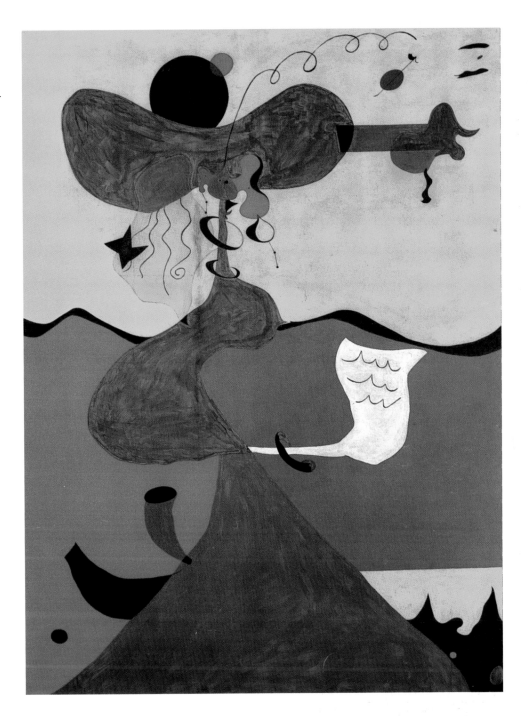

sel motor is no longer recognizable in the Prussian queen, Miró used this machine in a Dadaistic sense that assumes a somewhat sinister and martial aspect. The strong colour contrasts and the figure's floating quality emit an unspoken tension that makes this image one of Miró's strongest paintings.

In 1928 and 1929, Miró painted several metamorphoses of existing female portraits, using two-dimensional sources as inspiration. Perhaps he only had eyes for one woman in real life. In October of 1929, Joan Miró was married to Pilar Juncosa in Palma de Majorca. Nine months later in July of 1930, his first and only child was born in Barcelona, a daughter whom he gave the name of his sister and mother, Dolores. In August, the dictatorship of Primo de Rivera was ended and during the following year a young Spanish Republic was born as well.

New Constellations

Portrait of Joan Miró, Malaga, around 1935

After the Second Spanish Republic had been declared, the problem of Catalonia's nationality became partially solved. In September of 1932, the region succeeded in acquiring autonomic status with its own government, a parliament and extensive rights in running its own state bureaucracy. This was also the year that Miró decided to return to Barcelona, although for mostly financial reasons. In Paris, the Surrealist group had floundered and split. Miró had gradually drifted away from them, their disagreements and politics. With a wife and child, Parisian life had become decidedly more difficult and more expensive, its social life distracting rather than inspiring. In Barcelona, Miró and his family lived in his childhood home, with trips to Montroig and occasionally to Paris. The art market was suffering badly from the world economic crisis and by 1932, Miró's Parisian gallerist, Pierre Loeb, could no longer buy or sell all of his paintings. Thus Loeb asked Pierre Matisse in New York to help by taking on half of Miró's production in return for an artist's monthly salary. This must have been discouraging for the almost forty-year-old Miró. Although Miró had become successful in intellectual and artistic circles, and had been given one-man shows and included in group exhibitions, although he had done book illustration and worked as stage and costume designer, he still could not live from his art. By returning to his mother's house in Barcelona (his father had died in 1926), he could at least better his financial state somewhat.

As many of his contemporaries were also doing, Miró continued his experiments with media and materials. He made assemblages from found materials and objects; he painted, drew and collaged on paper, masonite, wood, sandpaper, copper. He was a painter who was trying to get beyond painting, to escape from purely visual experience and to lead his art in a more conceptual direction with a systematic approach. It would be hard to pinpoint exactly where he was trying to go, since he really did not even know himself. At times he felt destructive and angry about the limitations of painting. In 1933, working in the attic of his mother's house, he made a series of eighteen paintings that used collages as models. Similar to his choice of the diesel motor for the *Queen Louisa of Prussia* (ill. p.52), he again took pictures of machines and everyday objects from catalogues and newspapers and arranged and glued them onto a paper background. Miró saved the collages, yet they were not finished images in themselves, but preliminary states of paintings much as drawings might be. (Picasso also used collages this way.) According to Jacques Dupin, Miró purposely took non-poetic objects to force himself to work "against the grain" by denaturing the technoid objects into signs and figures of his organic world.[46] Miró was trying to halt his production somewhat and return to a constructed image, while

Ciphers and Constellations, in Love with a Woman, 1941
From January 21st 1940 to December 12th 1941 Miró worked on the series entitled *Constellations*, a small series of 23 gouaches and turpentine-colour paintings on paper. A host of stars, suns, and moons covers the surface linked by a network of lines.

Painting, 1933

preserving his inventive powers – perhaps he had grown distrustful of his own inflationary production. Doubtless the original meaning of the tools and machines remained somehow connected to the final image, although they were no longer recognizable in their original form. Perhaps one should imagine them as blanketed silhouettes of real things that assume an incognito. Miró seems not to want to lose touch with the cold technological world and at least preserve its memory, if not its face, in his work.

Although his work of the thirties was all in all less anecdotal, with a broader, simpler vocabulary of signs, Miró remains obligingly readable. For example, *Painting* of 1933 (ill. p.56) has made the collaged objects into little creatures that correspond to the original illustrations of tools roughly in shape, but not in meaning. Perhaps the small implements expanded upon here were related to the stage props Miró had designed for the Russian Ballet's production of "Children's Games" that he worked on a year before. (Léonide Massine had hired him to design the curtain, sets, costumes and accessories of the dancers. The art work actually influenced the choreography.) By making the tools of *Painting* into small beings on a stage, they became dancers themselves. *Painting* from

Composition, 1933

The pictures on this page belong to a series of large-format paintings produced from paper collages. The cut-out collage parts were transformed by Miró into bright colours. This series of pictures represents some of his most abstract work.

Painting, 1933

Painting, 1934
The small picture is painted on sandpaper, illustrating Miró's preference for unusual surfaces. The soft forms are reminiscent of contemporary paintings by Jean Arp and of his own work of the previous year.

1933 might not seem particularly aggressive, yet Miró, who had boxed for a while with Ernest Hemingway, used fighting terms to describe his work around this time, including the ballet job of 1932. "I am treating everything the same as my latest work: the curtain, the first 'hook' that hits the audience, like this summer's paintings, with the same aggressiveness and violence. This is followed by a rain of swings, uppercuts, and rights and lefts to the stomach, and throughout the entire event – a round that lasts about twenty minutes – objects keep appearing, moving and being dismantled on stage."[47]

Aggression, dismantling changes, sudden appearances and disappearances of reforms also marked, or rather marred, the first years of the Republic. However, Miró, who lead a peaceful and privileged life within his family, could still paint an image like the large, brilliantly coloured *Swallow/Love* (ill. p.59) in the winter of 1933/34, which was the design for a wall tapestry. Miró again employs poetic suggestions. Giacometti, who was a close friend of Miró around the time this picture was executed, later said, "For me, Miró was synonymous with freedom – something more aerial, more liberated, lighter than anything I had ever seen before."[48]

Yet as time went on, even Miró could not help but see the political developments around himself as a frightening whirlpool that might enlarge and suck everything down. His art and his letters voice these fears. The precarious foundation for political reform in Spain is revealed clearly by the civil-war-like events in October of 1934. There had been an election victory for the conservatives, which was answered by the Left with general strikes. In Catalonia and Asturia, the Spanish government reacted by declaring a state of war, which led to a social revolt that was quickly crushed in Catalonia. In Asturia, however, about 30 thousand miners resisted the Africa Army and the Foreign Legion commanded by Francisco Franco for two weeks. After the revolt ("Unite, proletarian brothers!") had been broken, about ten thousand "suspects" were arrested. The young Second Spanish Republic was doomed by the oligarchy's lack of support, and its unwillingness to give up its privileges, and by the desertion of the agrarian and industrial working classes, who were disappointed in their essentially unchanged situations. The intended balance that could not be accomplished through peaceful, reformatory means became a violent see-sawing of reactions that ended 1936 in civil war.

Miró's part in this world was that of an observer; as always, he did not openly talk about the crisis situation in Spain. Instead, he began what he called his "wild" pictures. *Woman* of 1934 is typical of a number of images of pained, startled or beast-like individuals, particularly women, executed during this period. Unlike earlier figures which were almost always composed of monochrome building parts, *Woman*, has been shaded, suggesting something more of volume, but also of discord. Her pelvis is a greying white with a tipped sexual opening and a tailbone, her upper torso an illogical asymmetry of intensive colour patches that vaporize into blues and whites, as if the figure were expelling a cry. (This change in the use of colour may have been influenced by the medium of pastel, which Miró used for *Woman* and a number of pictures to follow.) Her arms clamp her into her own suffering, while her horns and teeth make her seem out of control, certainly not an easy creature to calm and help. She once stood alone on a background that must have seemed too empty and solitary to Miró, for he filled in the space around her and between her arms and body with rough squarish groupings of scratch-like, thin, dark lines. These

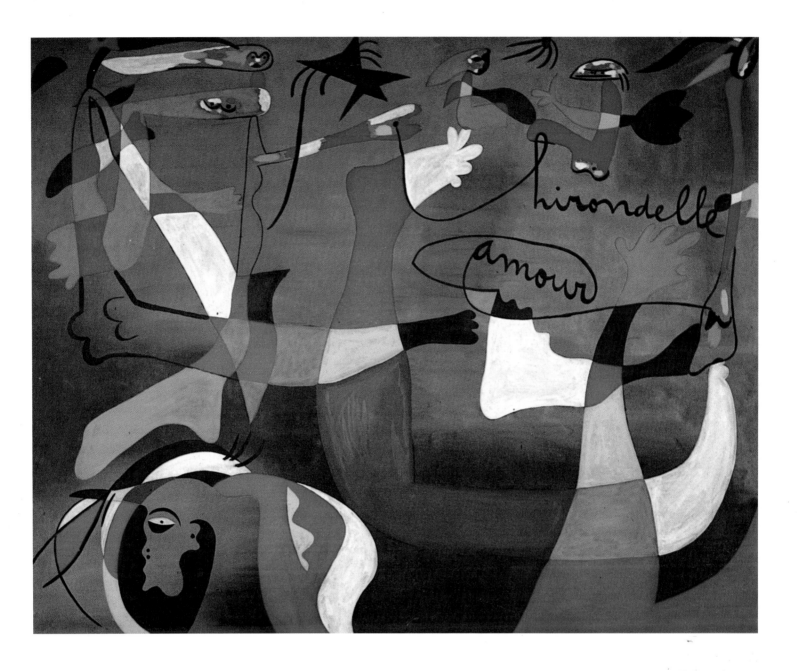

space fillers are made of mostly vertical and horizontal lines that slice through each other at approximately right angles. The line groups remain transparent, but suggest buzzing, shadowy centres around the woman.

Other images, like the oil paintings *Man and Woman in Front of a Pile of Excrement*, 1936 (ill. p. 63) or *The Farmer's Meal*, 1935 show more characters involved with each other in a science-fiction-like landscape or windowless interior space. Their inventive forms, heightened by extreme colour contrasts, express hysteric urges and reactions. Here Miró reveals the kind of unsurpressed associative Gestalt-perception that small children have before they learn to rationally disassociate: a hand may become a hook, a hammer and a knife, while cheeks may become tears, jowls and ears. In general, art historians interpret the emotional ambiance of the "wild" pictures as seismographic, communicating the shudders of pre-civil war Spain. Sometimes Miró projects this tension onto naked male and female figures, so that the problem seems to exist between the sexes and not between classes and political parties. Never do the "wild" pictures address specific events or issues, which holds them at least an arm's length away from becoming critical political art.

Swallow/Love, 1934
As early as the twenties, Miró had begun to experiment with picture poems. Here figures and word elements are linked by twisting lines: the word "hirondelle" and "amour" stand in front of the blue background as if written in the sky by an aeroplane or by the flight of a swallow. The free distribution of parts of the body and forms creates an effect of liberation and openness, birds flight and the free fall of one (or two) person(s).

Rope and People I, 1935
This picture begins Miró's so-called "wild pictures" of the mid-thirties which show a horror scenario. Man Ray points to the fact that Miró's use of the rope could have something to do with his own frightening experience of a threatened hanging in Max Ernst's studio (cf. Preface, p. 7).

Rope and People I from 1935 (ill. p. 60) is a collage that continues the "wild" pictures. Four vertical figures fill the vertical image: a man biting his own hand, a rope looping out towards his neck and two bare-breasted women. Miró, who saw the rope as constricting and hurting the figures, used it as a symbol of violence. In his autobiography, Man Ray wrote that Miró's use of rope had to do with his own frightening experience of a prankish threatened hanging in Max Ernst's studio. In contrast, Jacques Dupin interprets the rope as a helpful farmer's tool for hauling and tying. Whatever its implications may be, the linear qualities of the rope are at home in Miró's images. Often the lines on Miró's paintings, drawings and collages look as if they had been traced from strings that were dropped and pushed into place. Miró never mentioned doing this, but Antoni Gaudí had used string and wire to illustrate his building ideas in model

Painting, 1950
Here the pieces of rope have been bound together to make large knots. They make a three-dimensional relief out of the picture, making it appear as a precursor of the later Combine-Paintings of Robert Rauschenberg.

Still Life with Old Shoe, 1937
Everyday objects serve as the motif: a bottle, a loaf of bread, an apple (with a fork stuck in it), and the shoe mentioned in the title. The glowing colour transforms these simple objects into an apocalyptic vision.

"The Civil War meant bombings, death, firing squads, and I wanted to record somehow this very dramatic and tragic period. But I have to admit that I was not aware at that time that I was painting my Guernica."
Joan Miró

form. Clearly the fluidity of the material rope is "tied" to the expressive flowing line. The thickly wound rope in *Rope and People I* is roughly anthropomorphic, with its twists and loops. It represents a character with which the human figures must interact. The next *Rope and People II* tips the canvas into a horizontal format, while the rope remains a middle point. The small figures made of lines, wipes, strokes and blots are distributed around it to create a balance. These strange canvases with their interest in the thick material of rope almost seem like precursors of Robert Rauschenberg's *Combine-Paintings.*

After the outbreak of the Spanish Civil War in July 1936, Miró returned to Paris where his family joined him one month later. He was to remain in exile in France until 1940. At first, without a studio or a place to live, Miró was forced to stay in a hotel. Because he could not paint, he began a journal in which he wrote poetry and prose. Margaret Rowell wrote about his poems, "Miró's images are a painter's images: disjunctive, frontal and colourful. It is clear that in both painting and poetry his process was identical. Indeed one might call these verbal images poèmes-tableaux, rather than tableaux-poèmes."[49] Examples of this poetry show it to resemble some of the best Surrealist writing by authors like Robert Desnos and Benjamin Péret, two of the poets he knew since his days in the rue Blomet. Reading some of these poems, written originally in French that often rhymed, does much to illustrate the associative freedom, the sexual and scatalogical overtones that distinguish Miró's painting.

By the beginning of 1937, Miró realized that he would not be returning to Barcelona for some time. Although he was soon able to move to a small apartment, his working conditions in Paris were very limited and he felt he could not continue the series of paintings that he had planned to develop. In January 1937 he wrote to Pierre Matisse, "Given the impossiblility of going on with my works in progress, I have decided to do something absolutely different; I am going to begin doing very realistic still lifes... I am now going to attempt to draw out the deep and poetic reality of things, but I can't say whether I will succeed to the degree I wish. We are living through a terrible drama, everything happening in Spain is terrifying in a way you could never imagine... All my friends advise me to stay in France. If it were not for my wife and child, however, I would return to Spain."[50]

Miró began to work on a still life that he would come to consider one of his most important paintings. He set up an empty gin bottle wrapped in a piece of paper with a string around it, a large apple with a fork stuck into it, a crust of black bread and an old shoe on top of a table and spent five months painting them. Since he had no studio, he worked on the mezzanine of Pierre Loeb's gallery. He also spent time drawing nude models at the Académie de la Grande Chaumière with students and young artists. *Still Life with Old Shoe* (ill. p.62) recalls some of Miró's early work in its recovered realism. Why did Miró desert the more individual and personal sign language that he had established over the years? Without becoming a social realist, he was trying to create a more readily understandable image of humble objects that stood for humble people. Of course, the objects do not necessarily belong together on a table top, but they do express a sense of poverty and anger, of loss and desertion. Heavy, predominant blacks and dark greens crowd in on the objects that have been modelled with intense pure colours, as if they were burning in a dark night. Miró wrote that he was looking for "profound and fascinating reality" and trying to create a work that could "hold up against a good still life by Velázquez".[51]

Man and Woman in Front of a Pile of Excrement, 1936
A strong light-dark contrast lends and unreal and close atmosphere to the scene. The pile of excrement of the title stands on the right of the picture like a statue.

"I had this unconscious feeling of a threatening catastrophe. Shortly before the rain falls, aching limbs and suffocating closeness. It was more a physical than a spiritual feeling. I had a premonition of a catastrophe that would soon happen, but I didn't know what it would be: it was the Spanish Civil War and the Second World War... Why I gave it this title? At this time I was fascinated by the words of Rembrandt, 'I find rubies and emeralds in the dung heap'".
Joan Miró

The Reaper, 1937 (lost)

Miró painted this mural for the pavilion of the Spanish Republic at the Paris World Fair. The monumental portrait of a Catalan peasant with a sickle in his clenched fist stands as a symbol of the revolutionary.

1937 was also the year of the Paris World Fair. The struggling Spanish Republic belatedly decided to participate and show what it had already accomplished, but also the tragic plight in which it found itself. The Spanish Pavilion of 1937 was a successful marriage of propaganda and avantgarde art and architecture, featuring the work of Picasso, Miró, Julio González, Alberto Sánchez Pérez and Alexander Calder. The pavilion itself was designed by Luis Lacasa and Josep Lluis Sert. The artists and co-ordinators of the project worked together at a feverish pace to complete the building, with its documentary photomontages, sculpture and paintings. It was for this building context that Picasso painted his *Guernica* (ill. p. 65), which referred to the first aerial bombing of defenseless civilians in Spain. The architect Sert convinced Miró to cover a wall that stretched over the height of two floors – Miró had never painted anything of this size before. He decided to make a monumental portrait of a Catalan farmer hold-

Miró working on ***The Reaper*** for the Paris World Fair 1937.

"In the present struggle I see, on the side of the Fascists, powers that have become out-dated, on the other side the people, whose great creative potential lends a strength to Spain which will amaze the world."
Joan Miró

Aidez l'Espagne (Help Spain), 1937
This poster was designed by Miró in support of the Spanish struggle for freedom. The figure clenches its hand to form a huge fist: crude strength against the enemies of liberty.

Pablo Picasso
Guernica, 1937
Picasso's Guernica was also produced for the Spanish Pavilion at the Paris World Fair.

A Dew Drop Falling from a Bird's Wing Wakes Rosalie, who has been Asleep in the Shadow of a Spider's Web, 1939
The two pictures on these pages belong to the so-called burlap series: Miró developed his typical world of figures on the coarse material, giving them poetic titles. At this period Miró was leading a secluded life dedicated to his art.

ing a sickle in his raised fist. *The Reaper* is clearly related to the "wild" paintings, and it closely resembles the design for a fund-raising stamp and poster against the Spanish Civil War that Miró drew upon request in 1937 (ill. p. 65). The reaper had been the symbol of Catalonia's loss of freedom to the bureaucratic centrism of an imperial Castile since the 17th century. The celotex wall panels of *The Reaper* disappeared or were destroyed after the pavilion was disassembled. Miró, however, painted at least nine other works during that same year on celotex, which was a main building material of the pavilion.

It is strange that while the other artworks were saved or recovered, Miró made no attempt to save *The Reaper*. (It would not have been unlike the artist to use the marks on the disassembled panels as the starting points for new compositions, although he never mentioned doing this.) It was the *Still Life with Old Shoe* (ill. p. 62) and not *The Reaper* that Miró would later consider his equivalent to *Guernica*. As can be read in the Catalan notebooks from 1940 and 1941, Miró was planning a large tragic painting that would be an answer to *Guernica*, but without what Miró considered Picasso's melodrama. It was a work that never got painted.

The *Self-Portrait* of 1937 shows Miró was "seeing stars" and he was soon to begin a series of paintings that came to be known as the *Constellations*. At Varengeville-sur-Mer in Brittany, a sort of artist's colony where one of Miró's benefactors, the American architect Paul Nelson, had a house, Miró began a new stage in his work that had its source in music and nature.

In an interview with James Johnson Sweeney in 1948, Miró recalled, "It was about the time the war broke out. I felt a desire to escape. I closed myself within myself purposely. The night, music, and the stars began to play a major role in suggesting my paintings. Music had always appealed to me, and now music in this period began to take the role poetry had played in the early twenties – especially Bach and Mozart when I went back to Majorca upon the fall of France. Also the material of my painting began to take a new importance. In watercolours I would roughen the surface of the paper by rubbing it. Painting over this roughened surface produced curious chance shapes. Perhaps my self-imposed isolation from my colleagues led me to turn for suggestions to the materials of my art. First to the rough surfaces of the heavy burlap series of 1939 (ill. pp. 66 and 67); then to ceramics –… After the heavy burlap series of 1939 I began a

The Escape Ladder, 1939
The escape ladder is a motif which can be repeatedly found in Miró's work. In the days of the onset of the Second World War, it may be understood as a metaphor for the search for an escape from threatening world events.

The Nightingale's Song at Midnight and the Morning Rain, 1940

Ill. p.68:
Painting, 1943
After the beginning of the war, Miró began a series of paintings, the ***Constellations***. Stars, moons, suns, and figures are linked to form a delicate and close-knit "cosmic" network of signs. He systematically alters the colours on their crossing of the lines: red becomes black, black becomes red. The result is a pulsating of the forms in the background. Miró continually emphasizes his difficult search for compositional balance while working on this series.

Andre Bréton on Miró's ***Constellations:***
"They belong together and differ from one another like the aromatic or cyclic series of elements in chemistry. If one considers them both in their development and as a whole, each of them assumes necessity and value like a constituent in a mathematical series. And finally they give the word 'series' that special meaning by their uninterrupted and exemplary sequence."

Study for:
Constellations, 1940

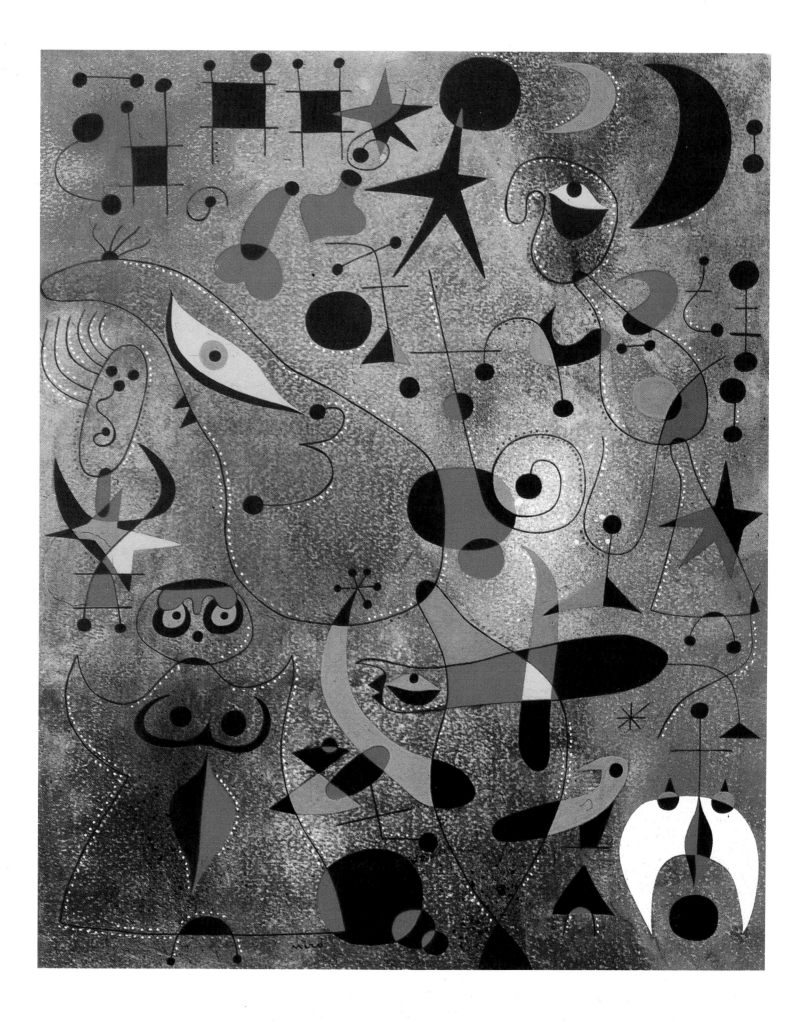

group of gouaches which were shown here in New York at the Pierre Matisse Gallery just after the war – an entirely new conception of things…They were based on reflections in water. Not naturalistically – or objectively – to be sure. But forms suggested by such reflections. In them my main aim was to achieve a compositional balance. It was very long and extremely arduous work. I would set out with no preconceived idea. A few forms suggested here would call for other forms elsewhere to balance them. These in turn demanded others. It seemed interminable. It took a month at least to produce each watercolour, as I would take it up day after day to paint in other tiny spots, stars, washes, infinitesimal dots of colour in order finallly to achieve a full and complex equilibrium."[52]

Just before the Germans occupied France, it was possible for Miró to flee and regain the comparative safety of his mother country. He continued working on these gouaches in Palma and Montroig. They were generically titled the *Constellations* after the completion of the tenth image in 1940. After this, the resemblance to astronomy maps increased somewhat. *The Beautiful Bird Revealing the Unknown to a Pair of Lovers*, 1941, uses linear tracery to link the dots defining the strange and amusing creatures staring out of the patterning. Limited areas are painted flatly in green, yellow, red and blue, however, the black of the dots, some hourglass or bow shapes and the lines dominate, floating clearly above a light surface that has been worked with washes and scratching to bring out its texture. Miró used the Surrealist method of letting the image come to him while working upon the "weathered" painting ground. Still, his source change from reflections on water to the heavens above is interesting. Perhaps he was reading Walt Whitman again, who, in his poem "Bivouac on a Mountain Side" contrasts the view of soldiers camping in a night landscape with the sky above them: "And over all the sky – the sky! Far, far out of reach, studded, breaking out, the eternal stars."

When they were shown in January of 1945, this series of 23 gouaches were the first new European paintings to be shown in New York for some time. Despite their small formats and their being executed on paper, (they had been smuggled into the country in a diplomatic pouch) they made a tremendous impression upon their audience. André Breton wrote the foreword to the catalogue, in which he calls attention to Miró's search for indestructable purity during the bitter years of the war. It was as if the art world were thankful that it had been possible for someone to have kept the flame alive.

The *Constellations* were to have a profound effect on the New York School of Painting and change the work of such artists as Arshile Gorky and Jackson Pollock. Miró's all-over distribution of forms, the variety of recurring elements, the application of automatic drawing principles and the idea of working in series began to blossom in American painting. These results would, in turn, be taken up in answer by Miró.

Of course, the influence of the *Constellations* was not untouched by the success of a major one-man exhibition of Miró's paintings in the Museum of Modern Art in 1941. Despite the war, it had been possible to mount the large show by using works from American collections. The catalogue mentions paintings, drawings, collages, objects, rugs, a tapestry and etchings. It lists Miró's contributions to stage design and book illustration, his prints, exhibitions of his work and a bibliography of articles about him. Although Miró could not go to New York himself, he had "arrived" there.

Women, Birds, Stars, 1942

Constellation: Awakening at Dawn, 1941

Constellation: The Morning Star, 1940

Ill. p.73 above:
The Bull Fight, 1945

Ill. p.73 below:
Women and Birds at Sunrise, 1946

Woman in Front of the Sun, 1950

Ladders Cross the Blue Sky in a Wheel of Fire, 1953

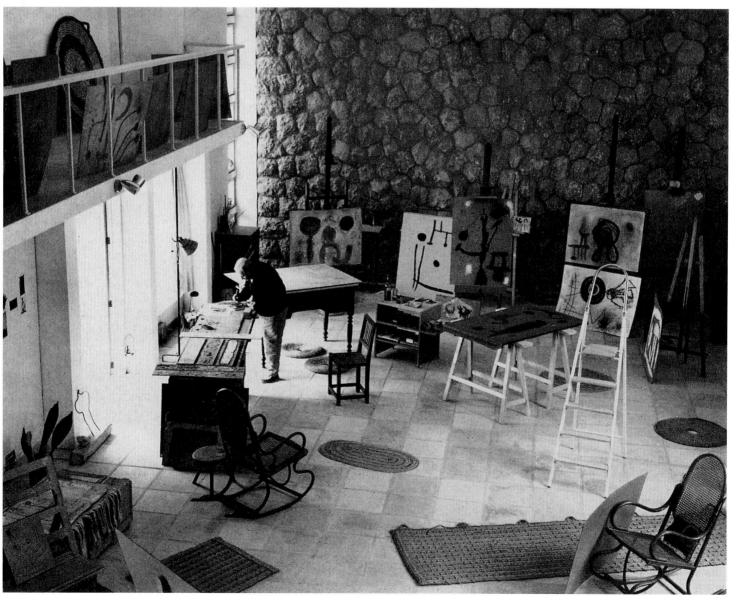

The Dream of a Large Studio

During the war years, Miró had worked to a great extent on paper, because materials were scarce and because paper could be more quickly and easily moved than canvases. He continued using a notebook to write down his ideas for art, so as not to forget them – and there were hundreds. Many of the ideas avoided using conventional art supplies, as if shortages were forcing him in experimental directions and reinforcing his interest in rougher materials. Besides his two-dimensional images, Miró worked with ceramics ("Take earthen jars like the ones from Felanitx and make little turds on them with a pastry tube"), branding irons ("Burn designs into the hides of mules or lambs, like the Indians did") and constructions ("May my sculptures be confused with elements of nature, trees, rocks, roots, mountains, plants, flowers").[53]

Many of the ideas in his notebook open out into the future, foreshadowing developments in Pop and Land Art. Yet the years of uncertainty made Miró worry about ever being able to accomplish enough during his lifetime. He needed more space and, at last, a permanent home. Already in 1938 Miró had a text published in the magazine "XXe Siècle", in which he voiced his wish for a large studio:

"My dream, once I am able to settle down somewhere, is to have a very large studio, not so much for reasons of brightness, northern light, and so on, which I don't care about, but in order to have enough room to hold many canvases, because the more I work the more I want to work. I would like to try my hand at sculpture, pottery, engraving, and have a press, to try also, inasmuch as possible, to go beyond easel painting, which in my opinion has a narrow goal, and to bring myself closer, through painting, to the human masses I have never stopped thinking about."[54]

During the last three decades of his life, Miró was to fulfill this somewhat contradictory wish to go beyond painting while at the same time getting closer to the common people through painting. Although it would remain Miró's main expressive medium, he would begin to take longer excursions away from painting by working with ceramics, printing and sculpture. At the end of the Second World War, Miró was not an ageing survivor disappointed by tragedy, but rather someone impatient to experiment and expand. It is not surprising that Miró should choose the end of the war to mark a turning point in his career. At 52 years of age he decided that he had to finally profit from his art. He wrote polite, yet business-like letters to his gallerists saying clearly, "What I will no longer accept is the mediocre life of a modest little gentleman."[55] Miró was aware that the time had come for him to exhibit and market his art more successfully than ever before. He needed financial success to establish for himself what he considered to be proper working conditions – the large studio – and make his art more and more well known.

In 1947 Miró travelled to the United States for the first time because his gallerist Pierre Matisse had secured a commission for him to execute a wall paint-

Catalan Peasant in the Moonlight, 1968
Miró's later work can be characterized by the simple use of a few pure colours. The pronounced use of the colour black is a new element.

Miró's studio in Palma was built by the architect Josep Lluis Sert. Since December 1992 it has housed a Miró Museum, whose light-flooded rooms still convey the impression that the artist has just gone out for a short moment.

Ill. p. 76 below:
Joan Miró in his studio in 1960.

Miró working on the Moon Wall for the UNESCO. Building in Paris around 1955.

ing for the new Terrace Plaza Hotel in Cincinnati. A huge painting was needed – 3 meters by 10 meters – and Miró worked on it for nine months in New York before it was shown there and then transported to the hotel for installation. While in New York, Miró often met with his artist friends who had spent their time of exile in the United States, most often perhaps with Marcel Duchamp. To execute the mural Miró used the studio of an American artist named Carl Holty. Holty later wrote an article about artistic creativity, which he published in the "Bulletin of the Atomic Scientists" and which discusses Miró's work on the mural. Holty was initially very disappointed in his encounter with Miró, until he rationalized his problem away.

"When the painting was almost complete and we were looking at it late one afternoon (after darkness made working impossible, for Miró was very orderly and punctilious about the working day), I pointed out certain accidental images of the mind that are bound to emerge uninvited in all complex fields of vision. Miró was not interested in these, nor moved to study the changes brought about in the painting by the waning daylight when the blues become lighter, the reds and yellows darker, and a painting often resembles a photographic negative of itself. I was surprised that all this meant nothing to him, the more since he told me that . . . he had tried out every manner of producing visual effects. But the real shock of the day came when I pointed to a large white form on the left part of the picture and asked, 'That is a fish, isn't it?' – and he answered somewhat irritably, 'For me it's a woman.' How was it possible that two painters, both of whom had painted non-representational pictures for more than twenty years (and I had once been much influenced by Miró's work), could be so far apart on such an important point? And how could we chide the layman for being so obtuse?

When I hedged a bit on my obvious misinterpretation by suggesting that perhaps he was more interested in the ornamental or decorative use of his 'private' language, he denied this, saying he was not the least interested in decoration or ornament but only in the image. What image then? He was not rigid about composition. While he did not change anything, he certainly added new elements.

One afternoon, after watching some children fly kites on the roof of our studio building, Miró was so inspired by the waving, undulating movements of the kite's tail that he drew those long rhythmic lines into his picture already 'equilibriated' and partially painted and right away without much deliberating. Since the canvas was so much wider than it was high, he drew the lines in horizontally in the lower right-hand corner of his painting, the only place where there was any room left. Surely, wavy lines running from left to right are not an exact interpretation of the vertical movement of those same lines leaping and soaring against the sky.

Perhaps the answer to what seemed so mysterious was given by another artist who came to look at the painting when it was finished. This visitor, who might have had some prejudices about Miró's work, in the presence of this painting was moved to say, with considerable emotion, 'It isn't true that he is a decorator. He is not at all decorative, he creates out of a spirit of visual wealth and imaginative opulence.' This seemed to establish the important image Miró created. It was an image of all that is rich and plentiful, singing colour, fantasy and poise. The rest, fish or woman, was perhaps a private matter."[56]

The viewer's ability to react immediately to the sensuality of Miró's painting has a lot to do with his or her enjoyment of it. (Of course, this also depends on being able to see the images themselves, instead of only reproductions of them.)

In 1968 Miró designed a large ceramic mural and labyrinth of sculptures for the Maeght Foundation in Saint-Paul-de-Vence.

"The splendour of the ceramics has guided me: it's like sparks. And then the struggle with the elements: with earth, fire… I am definitely a fighter by nature. When you make ceramics, you have to be able to tame the fire."
Joan Miró

Someone trying too hard to understand Miró's painting may not love it as much. On the other hand, someone very familiar with Miró's images may find it hard to keep being thrilled picture after picture, since his repetoire of forms repeats itself. The art critic Clement Greenberg, who met Miró during his stay in New York, had reservations about Miró's art, for he considered it marred by a decorative quality. However, he did feel that Miró had taught the world a lesson in "colour". He decided that Miró's art belonged to the Grotesque, as it was defined by the ninteenth century theorist John Ruskin: "Composed of two elements, one ludicrous, the other fearful." Greenberg becomes even more specific and classifies it as Ruskin's jesting Grotesque, since all in all he finds Miró's work more humorous than frightening.[57] Because Miró remained playful, it was difficult for some intellectuals to follow up their initial positive responses with total approval. American artists, however, were quick to respond to Miró's innovative painting techniques and he seems to have had a greater influence on postwar painting in the United States than Picasso.[58]

Another hotel, the Stanhope in New York, also featured a painting by Miró from which several individual motifs were taken and copied onto glasses, ashtrays and coasters. The simple designs, bright colours and black lines leant themselves to this kind of treatment. This quality – loved by some as basic express-

The Sun Wall, 1955–1958

At the beginning of the fifties Miró and his friend Artigas tested the possibility of using ceramics in his artistic work. In 1955 Miró was commissioned to design two long walls outside the newly built UNESCO Building in Paris. As a contrast to the concrete architecture around them, he designed two ceramic walls in intensive colours. One of these (ill. above) was dedicated to the sun, the other to the moon (ill. p. 78).

"And so the idea entered my mind that – to provide a contrast with the enormous concrete walls – I should put an intensive red disc on the larger wall. Its counterpart on the smaller wall was to be a blue crescent, in keeping with the more limited and intimate area.

I wanted to accentuate both shapes by means of vivid colours and clearly emphasized cut-out portions… I was trying to find some powerful expressiveness for the larger wall and a more poetic vein for the smaller one."
Joan Miró

His Majesty, 1967/68

iveness and maligned by others as decorativeness – predestined Miró to become an artist for the public space. In addition to painted murals, Miró was asked to design ceramic walls for buildings. During the war, Miró had begun working with his old friend and former fellow student Josep Llorens Artigas, who had become a master ceramicist. He was able to show Miró how to acquire the colours and forms he desired while using the unfamiliar medium. Since Miró insisted on working hand in hand with Artigas (as he did with all the technicians who assisted in his work, be they printers, weavers or foundry workers), he eventually learned a lot about ceramics himself. The medium was important to him as one used in folk art, for example, in the fabrication of the small Majorcan whistles whose whimsical forms inspired both Miró's painted and sculpted creatures. But it was also important to him because it was an earthen medium, belonging to no particular century. While working on a series of objects with Artigas during 1955, Miró was asked to execute two free-standing walls for the UNESCO building in Paris (ill. pp. 80/81). Miró, who took the chance to escape from more conventional object-making and immerse ceramics in his painterly imagination, chose the subjects of the sun and the moon. Collaborating with both Artigas and his son, Miró planned the work inspired by cave painting at Altamira, the rough wall of a Catalan Romanesque church and Gaudí's Güell Park in Barcelona, with its mosaic galaxies of sun and moon imagery.

The walls were 3 meters high and 15 and 7.5 meters long. Hundreds of tiles had to be made to fit together to form their surfaces. A first batch of geometrically shaped tiles failed. As Miró wrote, "This unfortunate experience cost us 4,000 kilograms of clay, 250 kilograms of enamel, and 10 tons of wood, not to speak of the work and time that were wasted." The second attempt with irregularly shaped quadrangular tiles was a success, creating the background upon which Miró was to paint his imagery. He did this "blindly", since the colours appeared only after the tiles were fired. Because some forms had to be done in a single gesture to keep their dynamic expression, Miró painted with a broom made of palm fronds. As he wrote in June/July of 1958:

"Artigas held his breath when he saw me grab the broom and begin to trace the five-to six-meter-long motifs, with the good possibility that I would destroy months of work. The last firing took place on May 29, 1958. Thirty-four firings had come before it. We used 25 tons of wood, 4,000 kilograms of clay, 200 kilograms of enamel, and 30 kilograms of colours. So far, we have only seen our work in pieces, spread out on the ground, and have not had a chance to step back from it. That is why we are so anxious and impatient to see the small wall and the big wall go up in the space and the light they were made for."[59]

The dominant *Sun Wall* (ill. pp. 80/81) and the more intimate *Moon Wall* (ill. p. 78) were greeted with much acclaim by critics and public alike. Miró's colours, signs, lines, and his moon and sun shone out upon the Place de Fontenoy in Paris, speaking to passers-by, whether they considered themselves an art public or not. His and Artigas' perfectionism, their insistence on the nuances, irregularities and texturing of the walls paid off. That year Miró was awarded the Guggenheim International Award, which President Eisenhower handed over to him in May 1959. What had begun as an experimental adventure ended as a stellar success. During the fifties, Miró bought a house and a piece of land on Majorca, where he had spent part of the war years with his wife's relatives. He commissioned his friend, the architect Josep Lluis Sert, to build him the large studio he wanted. The move to the new studio in 1956 meant consolidating his belong-

Fleeing Young Girl, 1968

Woman and Bird, 1967

Miró often made his sculptures from objects
and materials he found. He often put the parts
together as models which were then cast in
bronze. Finally Miró painted them in bright
colours: a series of works dating from the end
of the sixties give the impression of pop-
personalities.

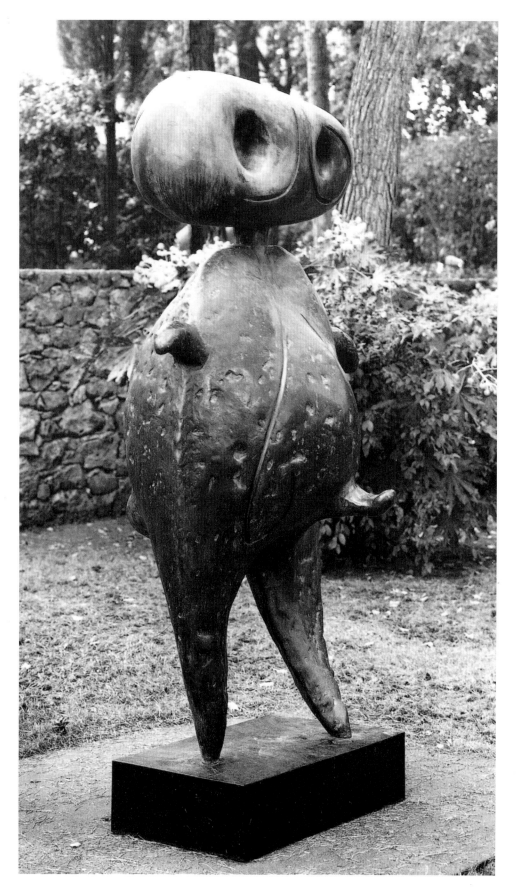

The bronze sculptures such as ***Insect Woman*** are often reminiscent of the older sculptor Alberto Giacometti. Other works seem to have just emerged from one of Miró's paintings.

Figure, 1970

ings, reviewing his ideas and destroying or overpainting things he felt were not worth keeping. The beautiful new space opened up many possibilities for Miró, who continued to work almost incessantly in a disciplined fashion. He travelled to Paris, worked with Artigas on ceramic projects, and went to the Maeght Foundation in Saint-Paul-de-Vence and to Barcelona to execute series of prints. The prints were important to Miró, since they were much less expensive than his paintings and brought his imagery into wide circulation independent of a museum context. It was one way of "reaching the people". He also began to make sculptures on a greater scale, which were sometimes cast in bronze at foundries in Barcelona and Paris. Sculpture appears to have taken Miró back to "things", back to the individual blades of grass, the insects, the rocks, the toys and the chance found items that he had always collected because they seemed meaningful to him. Miró made models for sculpture out of found materials, which could be either man-made, like a hat blowing along a beach, or natural, like a pebble.

Ill. above left:
Constellation, 1971

Ill. above right:
Insect Woman, 1968

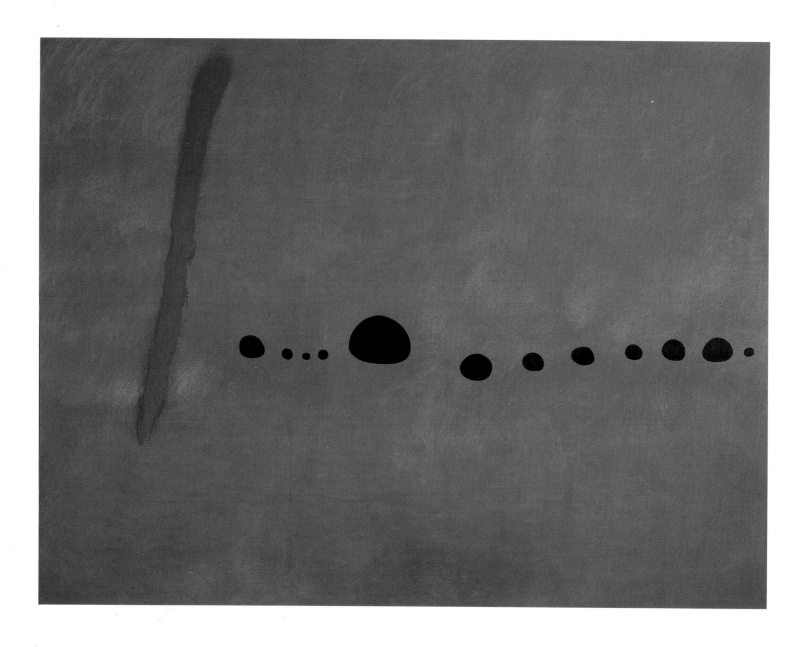

Blue II, 1961
The two pictures on these pages are part of a
triptych which Miró produced as a reaction to
his second trip to America. He had been
deeply influenced by abstract Expressionism.

In 1953 Artigas' son assumed the task of translating these constructions into
clay. Miró sometimes amended them. Besides such ceramic objects, Miró con-
ceived sculptures that were cast in bronze from modelled ceramic forms. Other
works were cast directly from constructed objects. The bronze figures might or
might not then be painted. Usually no or only very minor plinths lifted the sculptures up and away from the terrain of the viewer.

Miró's sculpture has many faces. During the late sixties, he made a great number of surprisingly fresh-looking sculptures whose humorous mixture of objects
and bright colouring made them into engaging Pop personalities: The *Fleeing
Young Girl*, 1968 (ill. p. 83), the *Woman and Bird*, 1967 (ill. p. 83), or *His Majesty*, 1967/68 (ill. p. 82) do not look as if they could possibly be the work of a
seventy-five year old man. Other pieces, such as *Insect Woman*, 1968 (ill. p. 85),
echo the sculpture of an older artist, Alberto Giacometti, in their rough surfaces
and verticality. Still others, like *Solar Bird* and *Lunar Bird*, 1966, or *Figure*,
1974, seem to be monumental tributes to Majorcan folk art, particularly to the
small handmade and painted ceramic whistles called "siurells", which Miró collected as early as the twenties.[60] And of course, some, such as the *Figure*, 1970
(ill. p. 84) or the *Constellation*, 1971 (ill. p. 85) could have stepped out of a painting by Miró himself. The sculpture park with labyrinth in Saint-Paul-de-Vence

might be the best place to see all types of Miró's sculpture in the place he liked it shown the best: outdoors. In 1962 Miró said, "All good sculpture should look immense in the open air. Moreover, I leave my sculptures outside. The sun, the wind, the rain, even dust improves them. Also, I often take my paintings outside to see if they hold up, to assess them."[61]

During the early sixties, Miró's paintings became emptier again, to the point where they resembled some of his work from 1925, when he executed almost monochrome canvases with only a few emphatic accents. One of several large triptychs, *Blue II-III* (ills. pp. 86 and 87), shows both clearly delineated and indistinct black and red forms against a bright blue field. The viewer is tempted to read the three canvases as the flying-saucer-like appearing and disappearing of the red bar. Time, space, orbits, but also microcosms invisible to the eye suggest themselves.

Miró produced the three paintings, which were sold individually, under the influence of his second trip to America. Pollock's Action Paintings and the abstract expressionism of Robert Motherwell and Marc Rothko had made a deep impression on him. Nevertheless Miro's forms are not of an abstract nature, even at their most reduced. They always remain endebted to nature which has inspired them.

Blue III, 1961
Joan Miró commented on these works: "It is important for me to achieve a maximum of intensity with a minimum of effort. That is why the empty spaces in my pictures gain increasingly in significance."

The Lark's Wing, Encircled with Golden Blue, Rejoins the Heart of the Poppy Sleeping on a Diamond-Studded Meadow, 1967

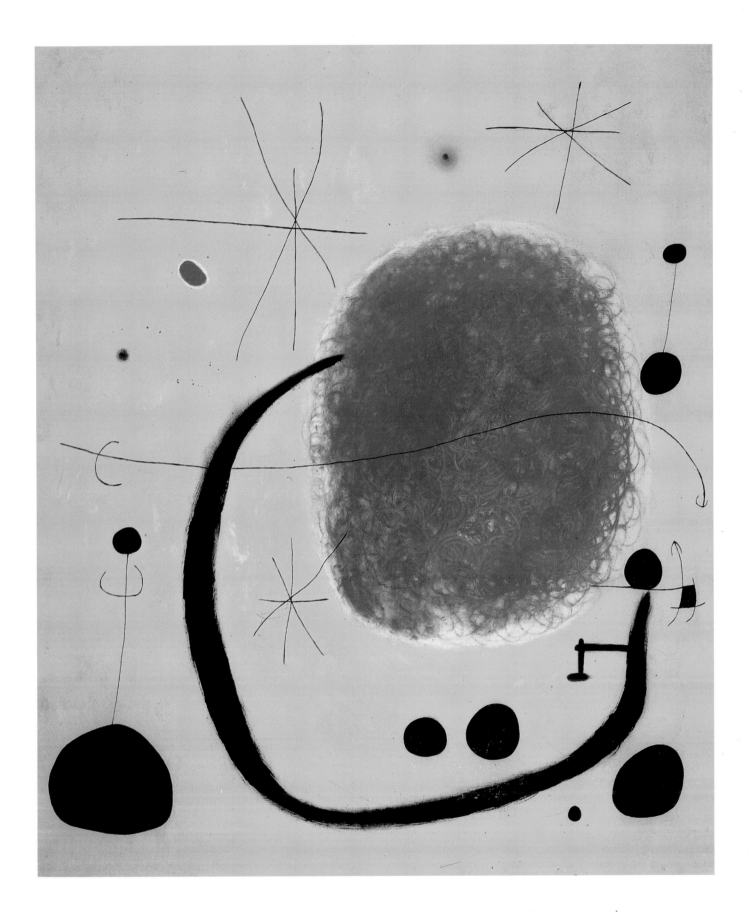

The Gold of the Azure, 1967

May 1968, 1973
The picture gives the impression of an obituary notice for the student protests of May 1968. The traces of the paint thrown at the picture, the contours of Miró's hands and the stunning colourfulness of the picture give no hint that he painted this at the age of eighty.

Over ten years later in 1973, he painted *May 1968* (ill. p.90), a delayed reference to the student revolution in Paris. It, too, recombines and recharges spontaneous gestures and deliberate signs and comes up with a painting that looks as if it could have been done during the eighties. At almost the same time, however, *Woman with Three Hairs Surrounded by Birds in the Night*, 1972, harkens back to Miró's idiom of the mid-twenties and thirties, even though the woman's skirt has a regular ornamental patterning that conforms only to more modern design. Miró was flexible in his imagery, reaching across time for appropriate impulses and inspiration.

Personages, Birds, Star, 1978
Miró once again intimates the elements that characterized many of his paintings. His later work adds a new quality to his world of signs, a far cry from the joyful figures of the previous years.

Miró had a colossal output. During his 90 years he made at least 2,000 oil paintings, 500 sculptures, 400 ceramic objects, and 5,000 drawings and collages. Using lithography, etching and other graphic techniques he created about 3,500 images, which were mostly published in editions of fifty to seventy-five. And all of them contain something of Miró's Catalan home, expressed by the language he developed in time, always growing from his roots there.

In 1936, Miró wrote, "Today, my young contemporaries know how to struggle when they are poor, but all that stops the moment they balance their budgets. Compared to these people who begin their shameful decline at the age of thirty, how much I admire artists like Bonnard or Maillol. These two will continue to struggle until their last breath. Each year of their old age marks a new birth. The great ones develop and grow as they get older."[62] Obviously Miró had disciplined himself into becoming just such an artist who would struggle, learn and develop as long as he lived, without compromising his own style. He would continue to make vibrant art without worrying about its contemporary correctness. The railway sign that Miró had once found in a shop and hung on his studio door in Paris because it had so appealed to him was quite correct: "THIS TRAIN MAKES NO STOPS."

Joan Miró 1893–1983: Life and Work

1893 April 20: Joan Miró Ferra born in Barcelona. Miró's father was a goldsmith and watchmaker, his mother the daughter of a cabinet-maker.

1897 May 2: Joan Miró's only sister, Dolores, born in Barcelona.

1900 Begins schooling and has first drawing lessons. Now spends the summers with paternal grandparents in Cornudella (province of Tarragona) and with maternal grandmother in Majorca.

1907 Miró's father persuades him to take business classes, which he attends dutifully. However he also has art instruction at the renowned academy La Escuela de la Lonja. His teachers were Modesto Urgell Inglada, a landscapist, and José Pasco Merisa, professor of decorative arts.

1910–11 Works as a bookkeeper for a hardware and chemical company. Illness and breakdown convince father that Miró is unsuited for business. Purchase of family farm in Montroig (province of Tarragona).

1912 Barcelona, April 20 – May 10: Exhibition of Cubist painting at the gallery Dalmau, with paintings by Duchamp, Gleizes, Gris, Laurencin, Le Fauconnier, Léger and Metzinger.
Begins studies with Francesc D'A. Galí Fabra (until 1915). Meets Josep Llorens Artigas, Enric C. Ricart Nin and Josep F. Ràfols Fontanals, with whom he will remain friends for the rest of his life.

1913 Enrolls in the Cercle Artístic de Sant Lluc for drawing classes (until 1918). Shows three paintings in an exhibition of the Sant Lluc circle.

1914 Rents studio with Ricart.

1915 From October – December fulfills required military service (every year through 1917).

1916 Gets to know art dealer Josep Dalmau.

1917 Dalmau introduces Miró to Picabia. Reads Apollinaire's poetry during final military service.

1918 First one-man exhibition at Dalmau's gallery (64 paintings and drawings). Founds "Agrupació Courbet" together with other artists.

1920 Early March: Miró's first trip to Paris. Visits museums and Picasso's studio. Draws at the Académie Chaumière. Attends Dada festival, Salle Gaveau.
Has three paintings included in Dalmau's show "Avant-garde French Art" along with works by Picasso, Severini, Signac, Metzinger, Laurencin, Matisse, Gris, Braque, Cross, Dufy, Van Dongen and others.
Catalan art show in Paris exhibits two paintings of his.

1921 Second trip to Paris. Paints in a studio rented to him by catalan sculptor Pablo Gargallo at 45 Rue Blomet, where André Masson is his neighbour.
First one-man exhibition in Paris, organized by Dalmau.

1922 *The Farm* is shown at the Salon d'Automne in November-December.

1924 Miró meets Paul Eluard, André Breton and Louis Aragon. First Surrealist Manifesto published.

1925 First one-man exhibition at Galerie Pierre. Impressed by Paul Klee's work at an exhibition in Paris.
November: exhibits in "La Peinture Surréaliste" at the Galerie Pierre and is invited to the surrealist banquet for St. Pol Roux.

Miró at the age of 18 months

1926 Max Ernst and Miró work on the set of the Ballets Russes production of "Romeo and Juliet".
Death of Miró's father at Montroig.
Has two paintings in "Exhibition of International Modern Art" in Brooklyn, New York.

1927 Miró moves to Cité des Fusains, with neighbours Max Ernst, Jean Arp, Pierre Bonnard and others.

1928 Trips to Holland and Belgium. First trip to Madrid. Meets Alexander Calder in Paris.

1929 October: Marries Pilar Juncosa in Palma de Majorca.
Returns to Paris and moves to Rue François Mouthon.

1930 Several one-man exhibitions in Paris. Included in "La peinture au défi" at Galerie Goemans.
Birth of only child, a daughter, Dolores, in Barcelona. First one-man show in the United States, Valentine Gallery, New York.
Included in exhibition of paintings with Masson, Ernst, Man Ray on the occasion of the premier of Luis Buñuel's "L'Age d'Or" in Paris. Exhibited works attacked by right-wing demonstrators.
First lithographs for Tzara's "L'arbre des voyageurs".
Becomes acquainted with the gallerist Pierre Matisse.

1932 Miró moves back into the home of his childhood, living and working on the top floor. There he designs costumes, sets and props for the Ballets Russes de Monte Carlo production of "Jeux d'enfants".

1933 Meets Kandinsky.

1936 Outbreak of Spanish Civil War. Visits to London and Paris, where he is caught in November by political developments in Spain. His family must join him there in December.
First monograph on Miró published, by Shuzo Takiguchi (in Japanese).

1937 Paints *The Reaper* (now lost) for Spanish republican pavilion, Paris World Fair.
From November to January, Miró and daughter Dolores sit for portrait by Balthus.

1938 Because he cannot go to Montroig, Miró spends summer in Varengeville-sur-Mer, Normandy, in house lent to him by the architect Paul Nelson. Paints fresco *Birth of the Dolphin* on the living-room walls.

1939 Paris. January: Franco's troops occupy Barcelona.
Rents Villa "Clos des Sansonnets" in Varengeville.

1940 Friendly with Georges Braque. Begins series of gouaches *Constellations*.

Miró with an Objet Trouvé, Montroig, 1954

1941   First large retrospective show, Museum of Modern Art, New York; organization and catalogue by James Johnson Sweeney.

1944   Miró's mother dies.
First ceramic works with Llorens Artigas and first bronze sculptures.

1946   "Four Spaniards" exhibition in Boston, Institute of Contemporary Art with Dalí, Gris, Picasso.

1947   First visit to the United States to execute mural for Cincinnati Terrace Hilton Hotel. Works on it during nine months in New York in the studio of Carl Holty.
Thomas Bouchard films him painting.
Meets Clement Greenberg and Jackson Pollock.
Asked to illustrate Paul Eluard's "A toute épreuve".
Does illustration for Tristan Tzara's "Antitête".

1950   Paints mural for Harkness Graduate Center dining room at Harvard University, Cambridge, commissioned by Walter Gropius.

1952   Miró visits Paris and sees Jackson Pollack exhibition.
Retrospective show in the Kunsthalle Basle.

1953   Starts work in Gallifa with Llorens Artigas on large series of ceramics.

1954   Venice Biennial, grand prize for graphic work.

1955   Invited to do two walls for UNESCO headquarters, Paris.
Included in the documenta I, Kassel.

1956   Miró moves to Palma de Majorca into villa designed by friend, the architect Josep Lluis Sert. Sells his childhood home in Barcelona. Begins work on ceramic mural for UNESCO Building.

1957   Miró goes to Altamira to see cave paintings with Artigas as inspiration for UNESCO walls.
Begins work with Jacques Dupin on major monograph.

1958   Completes UNESCO walls.

1959   Retrospective show, New York, which travels to Los Angeles. Miró makes second trip to the United States. Included in the documenta II, Kassel. Given Guggenheim International Award for UNESCO walls.

1960   Artigas and Miró work on ceramic wall to replace mural in Harvard Harkness Center dining room. Wall shown in Barcelona, Paris and New York before it is installed in building (1961).

1964   Inauguration of Fondation Maeght, Saint-Paul-de-Vence, with sculptures and labyrinth by Miró.
With Artigas executes ceramic mural for Ecole Supérieure de Sciences économiques, St. Gall, Switzerland.
Included in documenta III, Kassel.

1966   Artigas and Miró execute underwater ceramic sculpture *Venus of the Sea* for grotto, Juan-les-Pins.
Retrospective, National Museum of Modern Art, Tokyo, also shown in Kyoto. First trip to Japan. First monumental bronze sculptures.

1968   Honorary Degree, Harvard University. Fifth and final trip to the United States.

1970   Large ceramic mural executed with Artigas for the airport in Barcelona. Three monumental ceramic murals and water garden for the glass pavilion, World Fair, Osaka.

1975   Unofficial opening of Fundació Joan Miró – Centre d'Estudis d'Art Contemporani, Barcelona.
Death of Franco.

1976   Official inauguration of Fundació Miró.
Design for pavement "Pla de Os"; ceramic mural for IBM Laboratories, Barcelona.
Ceramic mural for Wilhelm-Hack Museum, Ludwigshafen.

1978   Catalan theatre piece "Mori el Merma" shown in European capitals.
Retrospective exhibitions in Museo Español de Arte Contemporáneo, Madrid, and Sa Llotja, Palma de Majorca.
Retrospective of prints, Madrid.
Two exhibitions of drawings, sculptures in Paris.
Monumental sculpture for La Défense, Paris.

Miró at work designing a frieze, around 1958

1980   Exhibition "Joan Miró: The Development of a Sign Language", Washington University Gallery of Art, St. Louis (also shown in Chicago). Retrospective exhibitions at Joseph Hirshhorn Museum and Sculpture Garden, Washington, DC (also shown in Buffalo, New York) and Museo de Arte Moderno, Mexico City, which travels to Caracas. Ceramic mural for Palacio de Congreso y Exposiciones, Madrid.

1981   Unveiling of monumental sculpture *Miss Chicago*, in Chicago. Costumes, sets for ballet "Miró l'Uccello Luce", Venice.
Unveiling of two monumental sculptures in Palma de Majorca.

1982   Unveiling of monumental sculpture *Personnage et Oiseaux*, Houston. Retrospective exhibition, Fundació Joan Miró, Barcelona. Unveiling of monumental sculpture *Dona i Ocell* (Woman and Bird) in Barcelona park.

1983   Unveiling of monumental sculpture in patio of government building, Barcelona. December 25: death of Joan Miró at Palma de Majorca. Buried in family vault, Montjuic Cemetery, Barcelona.

1992   December: Miró Museum opened in the artist's studio, built by Josep Lluis Sert, Palma de Majorca.

List of plates

44
Bathing Woman, 1925
Baigneuse
Oil on canvas, 73 x 92 cm
Paris, Musée National d'Art Moderne,
Centre Georges Pompidou

45
Photo – that is the Colour of my Dreams, 1925
Photo – ceci est la couleur de mes rêves
Oil on canvas, 96.5 x 129.5 cm
Private collection

46
Person Throwing a Stone at a Bird, 1926
Personnage lançant une pierre à un oiseau
Oil on canvas, 73 x 92 cm
New York, Collection, The Museum of Modern Art,
Purchase

47
Dog Barking at the Moon, 1926
Chien aboyant à la lune
Oil on canvas, 73 x 92 cm
Philadelphia (PA), The Philadelphia Museum of Art,
A.E. Gallatin Collection

48 above
Jean Arp
Stable Head, 1926
Painted wood, 61 cm high
Brussels, P. Janlet Collection

49
Landscape (The Hare), 1927
Paysage (Le lièvre)
Oil on canvas, 130 x 195 cm
New York, The Solomon R. Guggenheim Foundation

50 left
Hendrick Martensz Sorgh
The Lutanist, 1661
Oil on wood, 51.5 x 38.5 cm
Amsterdam, Rijksmuseum

50 right
Dutch Interior I, 1928
Intérieur hollandais I
Oil on canvas, 92 x 73 cm
New York, Collection, The Museum of Modern Art,
Mrs. Simon Guggenheim Fund

51 above left
Dutch Interior II, 1928
Intérieur hollandais II
Oil on canvas, 92 x 73 cm
New York, The Solomon R. Guggenheim Foundation,
Peggy Guggenheim Collection, Venice

51 above right
Jan Steen
Cat's Dancing Lesson
Wood, 68.5 x 59 cm
Amsterdam, Rijksmuseum

51 below
Studies for: Dutch Interior II, 1928
Etudes pour: Intérieur Hollandais II
Pencil, each 21.8 x 16.8 cm
Barcelona, Fundació Joan Miró

52 above
Queen Louisa of Prussia, 1929
La Reine Louise de Prusse
Oil on canvas, 82.4 x 101 cm
Dallas (TX), Algur H. Meadows Collection, Meadows
Museum, Southern Methodist University

52 left
Sketch by Miró on an Advertisement, 1929
Pencil

52 below
Studies for: Queen Louisa of Prussia, 1929
Etudes pour: La Reine Louise de Prusse
Pencil
Barcelona, Fundació Joan Miró

53
Portrait of Mrs Mills in 1750 (after Constable), 1929
Portrait de Mrs. Mills en 1750 (d'après Constable)
Oil on canvas, 115.7 x 89.6 cm

New York, Collection, The Museum of Modern Art,
James Thrall Soby Bequest

54
Ciphers and Constellations, in Love with a Woman,
1941
Chiffres et constellations amoureux d'une femme
Gouache and terpentine paint on paper, 46 x 38 cm
Chicago (IL), The Art Institute of Chicago.
All Rights Reserved

56
Painting, 1933
Peinture
Oil on canvas, 130.4 x 162.5 cm
Barcelona, Fundació Joan Miró

57 above
Composition, 1933
Composition
Oil on canvas, 130 x 162 cm
Berne, Kunstmuseum Bern

57 below
Painting, 1933
Peinture
Oil on canvas, 130 x 162 cm
Prague, Národni Gallery

58
Painting, 1934
Peinture-collage
Collage on sandpaper, 37 x 24 cm
Philadelphia (PA), Philadelphia Museum of Art,
A.E. Gallatin Collection

59
Swallow/Love, 1934
Hirondelle/Amour
Oil on canvas, 199.3 x 247.6 cm
New York, Collection, The Museum of Modern Art,
Gift of Nelson A. Rockefeller

60
Rope and People I, 1935
Corde et personnages I
Oil and rope on cardboard, stuck to a wooden board,
104.7 x 74.6 cm
New York, Collection, The Museum of Modern Art,
Gift of the Pierre Matisse Gallery

61
Painting, 1950
Peinture
Oil, rope and Case-arti on canvas, 99 x 76 cm
Eindhoven, Stedelijk Van Abbe Museum

62
Still Life with Old Shoe, 1937
Nature morte au vieux soulier
Oil on canvas, 81.3 x 116.8 cm
New York, Collection, The Museum of Modern Art,
Gift of James Thrall Soby

63
Man and Woman in Front of a Pile of Excrement,
1936
Homme et femme devant un tas d'excréments
Oil on copper, 23.2 x 32 cm
Barcelona, Fundació Joan Miró

64 left
The Reaper, 1937
Le faucheur
Oil on canvas, 550 x 365 cm
Lost, probably overpainted

65 above
Aidez l'Espagne (Help Spain), 1937
Silk-screen painting, 24.8 x 19.4 cm
Private collection

65 below
Pablo Picasso
Guernica (final version), 1937
Oil on canvas, 349.3 x 776.6 cm
Madrid, Centro de Arte de la Reina Sofía

66
A Dew Drop Falling from a Bird's Wing Wakes
Rosalie, who has been Asleep in the Shadow of a
Spider's Web, 1939

Une goutte de rosée tombant de l'aile d'un oiseau
réveille Rosalie endormie à l'ombre d'une toile
d'araignée
Oil on canvas, 65.4 x 91.7 cm
Iowa (IA), The University of Iowa Museum of Art,
The Mark Ranney Memorial Fund

67
The Escape Ladder, 1939
L'échelle de l'évasion
Oil on canvas, 73 x 54 cm
Chicago (IL), private collection

68
Painting, 1943
Peinture
Oil and pastel on canvas, 40 x 30 cm
Barcelona, Fundació Joan Miró

69 above
The Nightingale's Song at Midnight and the Morning
Rain, 1940
Le chant du rossignol à minuit et la pluie matinale
Gouache and terpentine paint on paper, 38 x 46 cm
New York, Perls Galleries

69 below
Study for: Constellations, 1940
Etude pour: Constellations
Pencil, 31.2 x 23.3 cm
Barcelona, Fundació Joan Miró

70
Constellation: Awakening at Dawn, 1941
Le réveil au petit jour
Gouache and terpentine paint on paper, 46 x 38 cm
New York, private collection

71
Women, Birds, Stars, 1942
Femmes, oiseaux, étoiles
Charcoal, pen, ink, water-colour and gouache,
90 x 43 cm
Private collection

72
Constellation: The Morning Star, 1940
Constellation: L'étoile matinale
Gouache and terpentine paint on paper, 38 x 46 cm
Palma de Majorca, private collection

73 above
The Bull Fight, 1945
La course de taureaux
Oil on canvas, 114 x 145 cm
Paris, Musée National d'Art Moderne,
Centre Georges Pompidou

73 below
Women and Birds at Sunrise, 1946
Femmes et oiseaux au lever du soleil
Oil on canvas, 54 x 65 cm
Barcelona, Fundació Joan Miró

74
Woman in Front of the Sun, 1950
Femme devant le soleil
Oil on canvas, 65 x 50 cm
Private collection

75
Ladders Cross the Blue Sky in a Wheel of Fire, 1953
Les échelles en roue de feu traversent l'azur
Oil on canvas, 116 x 89 cm
Private Collection

77
Catalan Peasant in the Moonlight, 1968
Paysan catalan au clair de la lune
Acrylic on canvas, 162 x 130 cm
Barcelona, Fundació Joan Miró

79
Ceramic Mural, 1968
200 x 125 cm
Saint-Paul-de-Vence, Maeght Foundation

80/81
The Sun Wall, 1955–1958
Le mur du soleil
Ceramic tiles, 3 x 15 m
Paris, Unesco Building

82
His Majesty, 1967/68
Painted bronze, 120 x 30 x 30 cm
Private collection

83 left
Fleeing Young Girl, 1968
Jeune fille s'évadant
Painted bronze, 135 x 50 x 35 cm
Private collection

83 right
Woman and Bird, 1967
Femme et oiseau
Painted bronze, 135 x 50 x 42 cm
Private collection

84
Figure, 1970
Personnage
Bronze, 200 x 200 x 100 cm
Private collection

85 left
Constellation, 1971
Constellation
Bronze, 142 x 130 x 44 cm
Private collection

85 left
Insect Woman, 1968
Femme insecte
Bronze, 108 x 21 x 18 cm
Private collection

86
Blue II, 1961
Bleu II
Oil on canvas, 270 x 355 cm
Paris, Musée National d'Art Moderne,
Centre Georges Pompidou

87
Blue III, 1961
Bleu III
Oil on canvas, 270 x 355 cm
Paris, Musée National d'Art Moderne,
Centre Georges Pompidou

88
The Lark's Wing, Encircled with Golden Blue, Rejoins
the Heart of the Poppy Sleeping on a Diamond-
Studded Meadow, 1967
L'aile de l'alouette encerclée de bleu d'or rejoint le
cœur du coquelicot qui dort sur la prairie de diamants
Oil on canvas, 195 x 130 cm
Private collection

89
The Gold of the Azure, 1967
L'or de l'azur
Oil on canvas, 205 x 173.5 cm
Barcelona, Fundació Joan Miró

90
May 1968, 1973
Acrylic on canvas, 200 x 200 cm
Barcelona, Fundació Joan Miró

91
Personages, Birds, Star, 1978
Personnages, oiseaux, étoile
Acrylic on canvas, 88.7 x 115 cm
Barcelona, Fundació Joan Miró

Notes

1 Man Ray, Self Portrait, Boston/Toronto, 1963, pp. 251–252
2 Interview with André Masson and Michel Leiris about Miró, in Apollo, Volume 127, March 1988, p. 190
3 Clement Greenberg, Joan Miró, New York, 1948, p. 38
4 See letter to Jacques Dupin from Miró about his childhood, in Joan Miró, Selected Writings and Interviews, edited by Margit Rowell, London, 1987 (Referred to in all following footnotes as "Rowell"), pp. 44–45
5 Ibid.
6 Ibid.
7 Ibid.
8 Miró, Letter to Michel Leiris, September 25, 1929, Rowell, p. 110
9 Cf. note 8 and also Miró in an interview with James Johnson Sweeney, Partisan Review, February 1948, reprinted in Rowell, pp. 207–211, see p. 208
10 Galí, quoted from Jacques Dupin, Joan Miró – Life and Work, New York, 1960 (Referred to in the following footnotes as "Dupin")
11 Cf. note 4
12 Robert S. Lubar, Miró's katalanische Anfänge, in Joan Miró, catalogue Kunsthaus Zürich and Städtische Kunsthalle Düsseldorf, 1986, p. 15
13 Miró, Letter to E.C. Ricart, Barcelona, October 7, 1916, reprinted in Rowell, p. 49
14 R.S. Lubar, cf. note 12, p. 16
15 Walther L. Bernecker, Sozialgeschichte Spaniens im 19. und 20. Jahrhundert, Frankfurt am Main, 1990, p. 233
16 Letter to E.C. Ricart, Barcelona, October 1, 1917, reprinted in Rowell, pp. 52–53
17 Letter to E.C. Ricart, Barcelona, May 11, 1918, reprinted in Rowell, p. 53
18 Cf. note 17
19 Miró, letter to E.C. Ricart, Montroig, July 16, 1918, reprinted in Rowell, p. 54
20 Miró, letter to J.F. Ràfols, Montroig, August 11, 1918, reprinted in Rowell, p. 57. In a letter to E.C. Ricart from Montroig, July 9, 1919 Miró indirectly compares himself to Walt Whitman.
21 Miró, letters to E.C. Ricart, Montroig, September 14, 1919 and probably November 1919, reprinted in Rowell, pp. 64 and 65
22 Miró, letter to J.F. Ràfols, Montroig, July 25, 1920, reprinted in Rowell, p. 74
23 Miró, letter to J.F. Ràfols, Barcelona, November 18, 1920, reprinted in Rowell, p. 75
24 Miró, letter to J.F. Ràfols, Paris, Hotel de Rouen, perhaps March 1920, reprinted in Rowell, p. 71
25 Miró, "Memories of the Rue Blomet", transcribed by Jacques Dupin, 1977, reprinted in Rowell, pp. 100–101
26 Cf. footnote 25, p. 101
27 Francesc Trabal, "A Conversation with Joan Miró", Barcelona, 1928, reprinted in Rowell pp. 92–93
28 Cf. note 27, p. 93
29 Ibid.
30 Lluis Permanyer questions Miró, "Revelations by Joan Miró about his Work" in Gaceta Ilustrada, Madrid, April 1978, reprinted in Rowell, p. 290
31 R.S. Lubar, cf. note 12, p. 12
32 Gabriele Sterner, Barcelona – Antoni Gaudí, Architektur als Ereignis, Cologne, 1979, this author's translation, p. 9
33 James Johnson Sweeney interview with Miró, in Partisan Review, New York, February 1948, reprinted in Rowell, pp. 207–211, see p. 207
34 Ernest Hemingway, in Clement Greenberg, cf. note 3
35 Gaëtan Picon, Joan Miró – Catalan Notebooks, unpublished drawings and writings, New York, 1977, p. 128
36 Rosalind Krauss and Margit Rowell in Magnetic Fields, Solomon R. Guggenheim Foundation, New York, 1972, p. 74

37 Miró, letter to Roland Tual, Montroig, July 31, 1922, reprinted in Rowell, p. 79
38 Cf. note 22
39 Picon, cf. note 35, pp. 72 – 73
40 Cf. note 37
41 Surrealist Manifesto, reprinted in Dada, Surrealism and Their Heritage, edited by William S. Rubin, The Museum of Modern Art, New York, 1968, p. 64
42 Miró in the Collection of the Museum of Modern Art, edited by William S. Rubin, The Museum of Modern Art, New York, 1973, p. 33
43 Miró, letter to Michel Leiris, Montroig, October 31, 1924, reprinted in Rowell, p. 87
44 Ibid.
45 Dupin, p. 179
46 Dupin, p. 239
47 Letter to Sebastià Gasch, Monte Carlo, probably March-April 1932, reprinted in Rowell, p. 119
48 Cf. note 42, p. 64
49 Rowell, p. 136
50 Miró, letter to Pierre Matisse, Paris, Hotel Récamier, January 12, 1937, reprinted in Rowell, p. 146
51 Miró, letter to Pierre Matisse, Paris, Hotel Récamier, February 12, 1937, pp. 146–148
52 Cf. note 33, pp. 209–211
53 Rowell, pp. 175–195
54 Miró, "I dream of a Large Studio", in XXe Siècle. Paris, May 1938, reprinted in Rowell, pp. 161–162
55 Miró, letter to Pierre Loeb, Montroig, August 30, 1945, reprinted in Rowell, pp. 197–198
56 Carl Holty, "Artistic Creativity", in Bulletin of the Atomic Scientists, volume 2, February 1959, pp. 77–81
57 Cf. note 3, p. 42
58 Barbara Rose, "Miró aus amerikanischer Sicht", in exhibition catalogue, Miro's katalanische Anfänge, cf. note 12
59 Miró, "My Latest Work Is A Wall", in Derrière Le Miroir, Paris, June-July 1958, reprinted in Rowell, pp. 242–245, see pp. 244–245
60 See Nicholas Watkins, Miró and the "siurells", in The Burlington Magazine London, volume 132, autumn 1990, pp. 90–95
61 Miró, Interview "Miró" by Denis Chevalier, in Aujourd'hui Art et Architecture, Paris, November 1962, reprinted in Rowell, pp. 262–271
62 Miró, Interview, "Where Are You Going, Miró?" by Georges Duthuit, in Cahiers d'Art, Paris, Nos. 8–10, 1936, reprinted in Rowell, pp. 150–155, see p. 150

The publishers would like to thank the picture archives, photographers, museums and owners for their contributions on the following pages:
Archiv für Kunst und Geschichte, Berlin 11, 65
Artothek, Peissenberg 36, 46, 57
Photograph © 1992, The Art Institute of Chicago. All Rights Reserved, Chicago: 54
Francesco Catalá-Roca, Barcelona: 76, 79
Colorphoto Hans Hinz, Allschwill: 2
David Heald, New York: 16, 38, 49, 51
© Photo R. M. N., Paris: 23
Philippe Migeat, Paris 73, 86
Kunsthaus Zürich, Zurich: 75